Baedeker Amsterdam

AMSTERDAM

Imprint

59 colour photographs
Map of Amsterdam, plus 24 other maps, plans, diagrams, etc.

Text: Karin Reitzig, with Birgit Borowski
Conception and editorial work: Redaktionsbüro Harenberg, Schwerte
English language: Alec Court
General direction: Dr Peter Baumgarten, Baedeker, Stuttgart

Cartography:
Gert Oberländer, Munich
Hallwag AG, Bern (city map)

English translation:
Babel Translations, Norwich

Source of illustrations:
Anthony (1), Artis Press Service (1), Beerman (7), Borowski (3), Diamond Center (2), Historia-Photo (3), Joods Historisch Museum (1), Dutch Tourism Bureau (19), Prenzel (1), Vergeer (7), Rogge (5), Sperber (9)

Following the tradition established by Karl Baedeker in 1844, sights of particular interest and hotels and restaurants of outstanding quality are distinguished by one or two asterisks.

To make it easier to locate the various sights listed in the "A–Z" section of the guide, their coordinates on the large map of central Amsterdam are shown in red at the head of each entry.

Only a selection of hotels, restaurants, shops, etc. can be given; no reflection is implied, therefore, on establishments not included.

In a time of rapid change it is difficult to ensure that all the information given is entirely accurate and up-to-date and the possibility of error can never be entirely eliminated. Although the publishers can accept no responsibility for inaccuracies and omissions, they are always grateful for corrections and suggestions for improvement.

4th edition 1991; completely revised

© Baedeker GMbH, Ostfildern-Kemnat bei Stuttgart: original German edition

© 1991 Jarrold and Sons Limited: English language edition worldwide

© 1991 The Automobile Association: United Kingdom and Ireland

© US and Canadian edition: Prentice Hall Press

Distributed in the United Kingdom by the Publishing Division of The Automobile Association, Fanum House, Basingstoke, Hampshire, RG21 2EA.

Licensed user: Mairs Geographischer Verlag GMbH & Co.,
Ostfildern-Kemnat bei Stuttgart

Reproductions: Golz Repro-Service GMbH & Co., KG, Ludwigsburg

Printed in Italy by G. Canale & C. S.p.A. – Torino

0-7495-0278-9 UK
0-13-094707-5 US & Canada

Contents

The Principal Sights at a Glance

Preface

This Pocket Guide to Amsterdam is one of the new generation of Baedeker guides.

These pocket-size guides, illustrated throughout in colour, are designed to meet the needs of the modern traveller. They are quick and easy to consult, with the principal sights described in alphabetical order and practical details about opening times, how to get there, etc., shown in the margin.

Each guide is divided into three parts. The first part gives a general account of the city, its history, prominent personalities and so on; in the second part the principal sights are described; and the third part contains a variety of practical information designed to help visitors to find their way about and make the most of their stay.

The new guides are abundantly illustrated and contain numbers of newly drawn plans. At the back of the book is a large city map, and each entry in the main part of the guide gives the coordinates of the square on the map in which the particular monument, building, etc. is situated. Users of this guide, therefore, will have no difficulty in finding what they want to see.

Facts and Figures

General Information

Amsterdam is the capital of the Netherlands, but the seat of government and the Queen's official residence are in The Hague.

Capital

Amsterdam is in the Province of North Holland, in the NW of the country.

Province

Its approximate latitude is 52° 50' N and its longitude is 4° 53' E. It lies above the deltas of the Rhine (or Rijn in Dutch) and the Meuse (or Maas) where the River Amstel flows into the IJ (pronounced "eye"), forming an inlet of the IJsselmeer.

Geography

The Dutch first rose to the challenge offered by their vast inland seas, whose beds could be 5 m (17 ft) and more below sea level, by using windmills to pump out four large lakes – Schermer, Beemster, Wormer and Purmer – in the 17th and 18th c. but it was not until the advent of steam power that they were able to tackle the Haarlemmermeer (Sea of Haarlem, 183 sq. km – 70 sq. miles) and the wide waters of the River IJ at Amsterdam. The process of "droogmakerijen", literally of "making dry", is a simple one whereby the water has a dyke built around it then is pumped away via purpose-built "ring"canals. The clay of the former lake beds is extremely fertile and makes very good arable land, equalled only by the most recent of the Friesian polders, whereas reclaimed marshland can only be used for grazing.

Land Reclamation

The greatest land reclamation project, made possible only by 20th c. technology, has been the poldering of the Zuiderzee (see Amsterdam A–Z, Zuiderzee), the vast inland sea formed by incursions of the North Sea in the Middle Ages. The narrow channel between North Holland and the island of Wieringen was closed off in 1924, and 1932 saw the completion of the "Afsluitdijk", the great dam that runs for 30 km (19 miles) between Wieringen and Friesland. Technically speaking, this was a gigantic undertaking because of the twice daily impact of the tides whereby the waters of the Zuiderzee exerted a progressively greater force within the narrowing confines of the dam advancing from both the NE and the SW.
With the completion of the Afsluitdijk, literally "the closing-off dyke", the Zuiderzee was a sea no longer and all that is left is the freshwater IJsselmeer. It is now relatively easy to fashion individual polders where the sea used to be, although this still entails a massive programme of all kinds of investment. The first stage was the drainage of the section between North Holland and the island of Wieringen (20,000 ha – 49,420 acres). The year 1942 saw the completion of the "Noordoostpolder", the NE polder (adjoining the Provinces of Friesland and Overijssel), and the first polder to be created in the Zuiderzee itself. The

Polders in the Zuiderzee

◀ *Amsterdam: city of canals and bridges*

Land Reclamation on the Dutch North Sea Coast

- 18th c.
- 19th c.
- 20th c.
- in progress

western part of the island fishing village of Urk was incorporated into the dyke. On the southern shore two polders have meanwhile been created. East Flevoland (54,000 ha – 133,434 acres) and South Flevoland (44,000 ha – 108,724 acres). A strip of open water has been left between the polders and the shore so that old coastal towns such as Elburg and Harderwijk still have access to the sea and the water table on the mainland can

Afsluitdijk Profile

High water mark
Average water level
Waddenzee
Embankment
Road
Stones
Stones
Clay
Sand
Ballast
IJsselmeer

10

Zuiderzee, the world's largest land reclamation project to date

be maintained at an acceptable level. The last of the polders was to have been Markerwaard (40,000 ha – 98,840 acres) off the coast of North Holland and due for completion in 1980, but because of opposition by environmental groups the government has withdrawn the plan for re-examination. This will still leave the IJsselmeer with a surface area of 110,000 ha (271,810 acres).

Draining the Zuiderzee is, to date, the world's largest coastal land reclamation project. The Deltaplan, approved in 1957, was another such project and brought a merger of the Islands of South Holland and Zeeland by closing off the open waters of the estuaries of the Rhine, Meuse and Scheldt; the construction of this dyke was completed in October 1986 (See Practical Information. Museums dealing with land reclamation).

Deltaplan

Amsterdam covers an area of 207 sq. km (80 sq. miles), 20 sq. km (8 sq. miles) of which is water, and, with about 680,000 inhabitants, is one of the main centres of the "Randstad Holland" (see p. 12). Population numbers declined in the 70's and early 80's but this trend now seems to have reversed.
As a conurbation Amsterdam, with its associated townships of Amstelveen, Diemen, Haarlemmermeer, Haarlemmerliede and Spaarnwoude, Landsmeer, Oostzaan, Ouder-Amstel, Uithoorn, Weesp and Zaanstad, has a population of about a million. The ancient nucleus of Amsterdam was Amstelredam, a 13th c. settlement on both banks of the Amstel. A grand project for expansion was formulated in 1612, part of which was the famous "Three Canal Plan". This semicircular belt of three canals (*Gracht* means canal) – the Herengracht, Keizersgracht and Prinsengracht – took shape in the 17th c., with the Singelgracht as the outer ring. The concentrically laid-out canals are

Surface Area and Population

11

Houseboat: taking to the water because of the housing shortage

traversed by a number of radial canals and streets ending in squares, thus dividing the city into about 90 islands joined together by a thousand bridges and viaducts. The only exception to this arrangement is the Jordaan district in the NW of the city.

Around 1800 there were approximately 21,000 people (1981 *c.* 35,000) living within the encircling canals in an area of about 800 ha (about 1976 acres). Between 1870 and 1900 the population doubled from *c.* 255,000 to *c.* 510,000 and the area of the city increased to 1700 ha (4199 acres), spreading beyond the historical ring of canals and giving rise to the "Volksbuurten" or workers' districts of De Pijp, Kinkerbuurt and Dapperbuurt.

A general reconstruction plan (lasting until the year 2000) was embarked upon after the Second World War. In 1951 a start was made on building garden cities. The overall plan envisages the built-up zones taking shape like outspread fingers interspersed with greenbelt areas. The garden cities were, in the W (around Sloterplas, a 90 ha (222 acres) man-made lake), Slotermeer, Geuzenveld, Slotervaart, Osdrop and Overtoomse Veld; in the S, Buitenveldert; in the N, Nieuwendam, Noord, Buikslotermeer and Buiksloterbanne (nowadays districts of Amsterdam; see Districts p. 14); and in the SE, Bijlmermeer (now called Amsterdam Zuidoost).

Although these new residential districts considerably alleviated the catastrophic housing conditions in the overpopulated inner city, the housing shortage is still acute. Today approximately 680,000 people live in the city of Amsterdam in an area of *c.* 21,000 ha (51,810 acres) and there are currently 53,000 priority applications on the official housing waiting lists. A small section of Amsterdam residents have made a virtue of

People in Amsterdam

necessity and taken to the water, where they live in some 2800 houseboats moored along the canals.

Randstad Holland, where many of the citizens of Amsterdam now live, is the generic term used to describe what has become a conurbation of townships encompassing the Dutch provinces of North Holland, South Holland and Utrecht. In the N it covers the area between the North Sea Canal zone and the southern shore of the IJsselmeer, and in the S between the Brielschen Meer, Alter Maas and Merwede. E to W it covers some 70 km (44 miles) and N to S it extends for 60 km (38 miles) and in that 3800 sq. km (1467 sq. miles) there live over 4 million people.

Randstad Holland

People and Religion

Randstad Holland can be regarded as having a N wing (covering Amsterdam, Haarlem, Haarlemmermeer, Zandvoort, Wormermeer, Zaanstad, Aalsmeer, Amstelveen, Weesp, Naarden, Bussum, Laren, Hilversum, Amersfoort Soest, Zeist, Maarssen, Vleuten-De-Meern and Utrecht) and a S wing (including The Hague, Katwijk, Wassenaar, Leiderdorp, Leiden, Leidschendam, Voorschoten, Voorburg, Rijswijk, Delft, Rozenburg, Vlaardingen, Schiedam, Krimpen aan den IJssel, Ridderkerk, Papendrecht, Dordrecht and Gorinchem).

Because of the concentration in this part of the country of industry, ports, commerce, administration and culture, as well as intensive forms of agriculture, the Randstad Holland constitutes the economic heart of the Netherlands.

Districts

The city is divided up into 30 districts (Wijken). These are: Admiralenbuurt, Bijlmeer, Buikslotermeer, Buiksloterbanne, Buitenveldert, Centuur, Concertgebouw/Vondelpaarkbuurt, Driemond, De Eilanden, Geuzenveld, De Gouden Real, Indische Buurt, Jordaan, Landelijk Noord, Landlust/Bos en Lommer, Muiderpoort, Nieuwendam, Noord, Oostzaan, Osdorp, Oude Stad, Oud West, Rivierenbuurt, Sloten, Slotermeer, Slotervaart/Overtoomse Veld, Spaarndam, Staatslieden/Frederik-Hendrikbuurt, Watergraafsmeer, Zuid.

Administration

The city is administered by a City Council consisting of 36 Councillors and nine Aldermen, chaired by the Burgomaster (or Lord Mayor). The Councillors, who elect the Aldermen from among their own number, are elected by the people for a term of four years. The Burgomaster is appointed by the "Crown" (the Queen and the Council of Ministers) for a term of six years. The City Hall (Stadhuis), the seat of the City Council, is in the "Stopera" on the Waterlooplein.

People and Religion

People

The people of Amsterdam reflect the population structure of the Netherlands. Many of those who were forced to flee their own countries for political or religious reasons and took refuge in the Netherlands came to live in Amsterdam. The Netherlands, and with it Amsterdam, continues to attract many foreign workers as well as citizens of the former Dutch colonies who share the general belief that better living and working conditions are to be found in the mother country.

Thus among the people of Amsterdam one finds Indonesians (9600), Surinamese and people from the Dutch Antilles (together about 176,000 in the country as a whole) as well as Britons, Americans, Germans, Spaniards, Moroccans, Yugoslavs, Jews, Armenians and Levantines.

Religion

After the Reformation in the 16th c. there evolved in Amsterdam, alongside the Roman Catholic Church, many Protestant sects such as the Evangelical Lutherans or the Amsterdam Reformed Church. The many refugees and other foreigners who settled in Amsterdam each brought their own faiths with them so that one finds a great many "imported" religions: there are Anglican and Presbyterian Churches and several synagogues, as well as places of worship for Buddhists, Hindus and Muslims.

Something of a general decline in the established religions has

The busy port of Amsterdam

coincided with a flowering of "alternative" religious movements. Amsterdam is very much a centre for some of these such as the international society for Krishna Consciousness and Scientology.

The city has various yoga and meditation centres, of which the best-known are Kosmos, Stichting Universum and Mozeshuis (in the Moses and Aaron Church).

Communications

Amsterdam's port and commerce are of considerable importance. The port on the S bank of the North Sea Canal has expanded in recent decades with new port installations and industrial estates to cover an area of 2725 ha (6730 acres). Although it lags far behind Rotterdam in terms of tonnage, because of its location between the North Sea and the highly industrialised European hinterland, its significance as regards the trans-shipment of freight grew after the Second World War, once the opening of the Amsterdam–Rhine Canal in 1952 brought it within easy reach of the European markets. The year 1876 had seen the opening of the North Sea Canal (270 m (886 ft) wide, 15 m (50 ft) deep and 15 km (9 miles) long) which provided a passage to the sea and was navigable irrespective of the state of the tide, thanks to the sluices at IJmuiden, part of the world's largest complex of sluices.

Port

From the 17th c. onwards the port of Amsterdam looked after the country's traffic with its colonies overseas, and the decades

Communications

Bikes – the Amsterdammer's favourite mode of transport

following the Second World War have seen it grow into an industrial bulk-handling port. It has a container terminal and up-to-date storage facilities, with a petrochemical tank complex capable of taking over a million tonnes. Every year several thousand ships are handled; the manufactured goods are destined for internal European markets, the raw materials for national and local industry. There are ferry services from Amsterdam harbour to Immingham (UK) and Göteborg (Sweden) carrying about 200,000 passengers a year.

Airport

Amsterdam's airport, Schiphol, which lies 10 km (6 miles) S of the city, is one of Europe's major airports. Over 85 airlines are represented, operating flights to more than 90 countries; on average Schiphol handles about 14.5 million passengers a year. Since 1986 the airport has been connected directly by rail (Centraal Station) with the centre of Amsterdam. Apart from its passenger traffic, Schiphol is an important distribution centre for valuable consumer goods, such as electronic equipment, and optical and medical instruments. Its annual freight turnover amounts to 758,000 tonnes.

Rail and Underground

Through the international rail network Amsterdam is linked to all of Europe's major cities, with the volume of freight traffic matching the number of passengers.
To reduce the daily flow of cars in the rush-hour it is planned to extend the network of rail commuter services; and the Underground, with two routes and 20 stations, that came into operation in 1977 is one example of this. Public transport within the city is also catered for by buses and trams.

Het Muziektheater *Concertgebouw Orkest*

A1	Apeldoorn–Amersfoort	Arterial Roads
A2 (E8)	Utrecht–Arnhem	
A4 (E10)	Schiphol–The Hague–Rotterdam	
A8	Zaandstad–Alkmaar–Afsluitdijk	
A9	Amstelveen–Haarlem–Zandvoort	
E35	Hilversum–Amersfoort	
N5	Haarlem–Zandvoort	

The bicycle is the most popular mode of transport (575,000 bikes among 680,000 residents), although it is never quite clear who owns which bike. *Bicycles*

Culture

Amsterdam is the country's cultural centre and the main seat of learning and science (including the country's largest university and the Dutch Academy of Science), together with teaching and research. It is the home of world-famous museums such as the Rijksmuseum, with its great collection of old masters, the Stedelijk Museum for modern art and the Van Gogh Museum. The Concertgebouw and the Philharmonic Orchestras are internationally famous and the National Ballet and the Nederlands Dans Theater are well known throughout the world. In 1986 the new opera house on Waterlooplein, Het Muziektheater, which is intended for operatic and ballet productions, was opened. It has a capacity for an audience of 1640.
Visitors come from all over the world to the Holland Festival every summer for its international programme of ballet, opera, music, theatre, folk-dance, etc. *General*

Amsterdam is famous for its diamond cutting

Amsterdam also has many art galleries and innumerable avant-garde music, dance and drama groups. The most important newspaper and book publishers are located in Amsterdam.

Academies

Amsterdam's many academies include the Architectural Academy, the National Academy of the Visual Arts, the Gerrit Rietveld Academy (for industrial design), the Dutch Film Academy, the academies for the performing arts, etc.
Also in Amsterdam are the Royal Dutch Academy of Science, the Royal Society for the promotion of architecture, and the Royal Dutch Geographical Society.

Universities and Research Institutes

The University of Amsterdam, founded in 1877, now has about 30,000 students. The University has eight faculties and, with its institutes, laboratories and training colleges, is one of the most important in Europe.
In 1880 the Dutch Reformed Church set up its own university in Amsterdam. The "Free University", as it is called, has five faculties with about 13,000 students.
Also in Amsterdam one finds the Catholic Theological College, teacher training establishments, two conservatoires and a great many research institutes (including the State aviation and aerospace establishment, a nuclear physics research institute, the Royal Tropical Institute, the International Archive for Women's Movements, the International Institute for Social History and the Institute of Journalism).

Libraries

Among Amsterdam's major libraries are the University Library (c. 2 million volumes), the Public Library, the art libraries of the

Stedelijk Museum and the Rijksmuseum, the Music Library and the library of the Tropical Museum.

Industry and Commerce

As the capital of the Netherlands and Europe's second largest port, Amsterdam is important for its trade and commerce, and is the headquarters of about 16,000 businesses, and some 8% of the country's international trade passes through Amsterdam. It is also the centre of the country's car trade and most of the well-known makes of car have franchises here.

Amsterdam, in the 17th c. the greatest commercial city in the world, is today, with its concentration of major banks and insurance companies, central to Dutch business life. Its stock exchange, one of the oldest in the world, is of international standing. Besides the Bank of the Netherlands there are also foreign and private banks.

8% of the city's earnings come from tourism. It is the fourth largest tourist town in Europe.

Centre of Dutch Commerce

In addition to its port (see Amsterdam A–Z, Port) and commerce, Amsterdam also owes its importance in the economy to the fact that it lies in the middle of an industrial belt stretching from IJmuiden on the North Sea coast as far as Hilversum.

The industrial development of the port after the Second World War brought about a shift in emphasis from the traditional shipbuilding and repair with the coming, in the western part of the port, of a giant chemical and petrochemical complex on the completion of the pipeline to Rotterdam. With as many as 15,000 industrial companies in all located on the new industrial estates in the W, SW and S of the city, Amsterdam is the largest Dutch industrial city.

The major fields of production, besides the fast-growing chemical industry, are motor and aircraft manufacturing, together with various kinds of engineering.

Amsterdam's diamond industry enjoys worldwide renown and was brought here by the diamond-cutters who fled the sacking of Antwerp in 1586. It is also the centre for the manufacture of wooden and leather goods, soap-making (one of its oldest trades) and the film industry.

Amsterdam has also long been the centre of the Dutch textile industry, leading the way in fashion and ready-to-wear clothing, and it is also an important producer of foodstuffs, confectionery and similar luxury products, with chocolate and cigarette factories, breweries, etc.

A large number of printing works points to the city's importance as the focus for the Dutch press, publishing and the book trade.

Centre of Dutch industry

19

Famous People

Karel Appel
(b. 25.4.1921)

Karel Appel, who was born in Amsterdam, is one of the most internationally famous and controversial post-war Dutch painters. He received his first major commission in 1949 – a frieze for Amsterdam City Hall entitled "Vragende Kinderen" ("Questioning Children") – which sparked off such a public outcry that the work had to be covered up for a time.

In 1950 Appel settled in Paris where he joined the international experimental school and was one of the founders of the COBRA group (Copenhagen, Brussels, Amsterdam) composed of artists now enjoying international acclaim such as Corneille, Constant, Alechinsky, Asger Jorn and Lucebert.

In the fifties Appel took part in many important exhibitions and received international awards and prizes, including the 1954 UNESCO Prize at the Venice Biennale and the Guggenheim Prize in 1960.

Karel Appel's work, much of which can be seen in the Stedelijk Museum, is characterised by an especially expressive and vibrant use of colour.

Hendrik Petrus Berlage
(21.2.1856–12.8.1934)

Hendrik Petrus Berlage was a brilliant and typically Dutch architect whose highly original style in the building that made him famous, the Amsterdam Exchange (begun 1897), marked the transition between historicism and the 20th c. A great influence on architecture both inside and outside the Netherlands, he was also responsible for the bridge over the Amstel bearing his name and the Gemeentelijk (Municipal) Museum in The Hague, while the furniture he designed assured him a prominent place in the field of applied arts.

Anne Frank
(2.6.1929–March 1945)

Anne Frank, a Jewish girl from Germany, achieved fame through her diary which has been filmed and translated into many languages.

The Jewish Frank family fled Hitler's Frankfurt in 1933 and came to Amsterdam where they went into hiding during the German occupation. Anne kept a diary on their life over this period (12 June 1942–1 August 1944) which ended when the whole family was discovered and transported to Germany. Anne, together with her mother and sister, died in Belsen concentration camp and only her father survived. After the Liberation the diary was found in the family's Amsterdam hideout and published.

Rembrandt
(Harmensz van Rijn)
(15.7.1606–4.10.1669)

Rembrandt, the most famous of all Dutch painters, moved to Amsterdam in 1632, after an early creative period in his native Leyden; in 1634 he married Saskia van Uijlenburgh, the wealthy daughter of a burgomaster. In 1639 he bought the house in the Jodenbreestraat which is today the Rembrandthuis.

During his first ten years in Amsterdam he was much in demand for his portraits, and almost two-thirds of all his commissioned work dates from this period. His portraits were true to life and made no concessions to flattery. Besides his impressive individual portraits (including Burgomaster J. Six), his group portraits ("The Anatomy Lesson of Dr Tulp") and

Joost van den Vondel   *Rembrandt*

self-portraits (with Saskia, the painter as the Prodigal Son), he also painted biblical themes and, later in life, landscapes.

As Rembrandt increasingly declined to subjugate the artistic integrity of his portraits to the wishes of his patrons, the number of commissions declined, and, in fact, the patrons who commissioned "The Night Watch" refused to accept it.

After Saskia's death in 1642 Rembrandt got into personal and financial difficulties and in 1656 was declared bankrupt. Titus, his son by Saskia, and Hendrickje Stoffels, his common-law wife, formed a company to help Rembrandt's financial situation but until his death he remained encumbered by debts, in growing artistic and social isolation (Rembrandt's "The Swearing-in of the Batavians under Julius Civilis" for the new Town Hall in Amsterdam was rejected and replaced by the work of one of his pupils).

When he died in 1669 Rembrandt was buried outside the Westerkerk and was only subsequently reinterred inside the church. Rembrandt left 562 paintings, 300 etchings and 1600 drawings. His best-known works are "The Night Watch" (1642), "The Anatomy Lesson on Dr Tulp" (1632), "The Staalmeesters" (1661/2) and "The Jewish Bride" (*c.* 1665), all of which are in the Rijksmuseum. His best-known self-portrait hangs in the Mauritshuis in The Hague, and almost all his etchings and many of his drawings can be seen in the Rembrandthuis.

The Dutch philosopher Baruch (or Benedictus) de Spinoza was born in the Jewish quarter of Amsterdam and given a Hebrew education. His independent thinking ran counter to Jewish beliefs and led in 1656 to his excommunication. A considerable influence on Western philosophy, he was above all a rationalist and set out to prove his metaphysical pantheistic doctrines by mathematical demonstration.

Baruch (Benedictus) de Spinoza (24.11.1632–21.2.1677)

His best-known work, "Ethics demonstrated by geometrical methods", written between 1660 and 1675, was not published until after his death.

Spinoza's house in The Hague was taken over by the Spinoza Institute in 1927.

Joost van den Vondel was the greatest poet of the Dutch Renaissance. His writings ranged from satirical, historical, patriotic and religious poetry to his 32 plays, of which the

Joost van den Vondel (17.11.1587–5.2.1679)

best-known are "Gijsbreght van Aemstel" (1637) and "Lucifer" (1654). He also translated the Psalms, Ovid and Virgil into Dutch.

Van den Vondel, who played an active part in the political and religious struggles of his times and was converted to Catholicism in 1641, died aged 92 in Amsterdam in 1679. The city's largest park is named after him.

History of the City

A dam is built separating the mouth of the Amstel from the arm of the Zuiderzee called the "IJ". | 1270

Floris V, Count of Holland, grants the people of the fishing village of Amstelledamme freedom from tolls on travel and on trade in their own goods within the County of Holland. | 1275

Amsterdam receives its charter. | 1300

The Bishops of Utrecht transfer the city to Count Willem III of Holland. | 1317

The city becomes the point where duty is levied on beer imported from Hamburg, thus leading to increased trade with the Hanseatic towns. | 1323

The "miracle of the Host" makes Amsterdam a place of pilgrimage, and pilgrims flock to the chapel built in the Kalverstraat in 1347. When Emperor Maximilian is cured of an illness while on a pilgrimage in 1489 he grants the city the right to bear the Imperial crown in its coat of arms. | 1345

The four Burgomasters are elected annually by the Council of Elders which gives the city relative independence from the country's rulers. | from 1400

The city of Amsterdam is almost completely destroyed by a great fire. | 1421

Building of a stone city wall. | 1481

The city is plunged into the upheaval of the Reformation. Anabaptists run naked in a state of religious ecstasy over the Dam and almost succeed, on 10 May, in occupying the Town Hall. The city fathers summon the aid of the Hapsburg Emperor Charles V. | 1535

The population of Amsterdam has grown to over 30,000. | 1538

During a famine churches and monasteries are stormed by adherents of the Reformation. Philip II of Spain succeeds to the throne of Charles V. | 1566

Duke of Alba occupies Amsterdam on behalf of Philip II and savagely persecutes the followers of the Reformation. | 1567

During an uprising by the Northern Provinces of the Low Countries Amsterdam remains pro-Spanish. | 1568

William the Silent, Prince of Orange, becomes the leader of the uprising against Spain. | 1572

After the city surrenders to William's troops, Amsterdam joins in the Dutch War of Independence from Spain. All pro-Spanish | 1578 civic leaders, clerics and clergy have to leave the city ("Alter-atie"). A new civic administration consists mainly of immigrant Reformed merchants. The "Satisfactie van Amsterdam" lays down that no one may be persecuted for their beliefs.

1578 onwards   Amsterdam becomes one of the most important cities for com-merce in the world, a centre for culture and science, a city with flourishing crafts and a cosmopolitan population. Refugees from the whole of Europe come to settle in the city.

1595–1597   A fleet, financed mainly by Amsterdam merchants, succeeds in finding a sea route to India round the southern tip of Africa.

1602   Founding of the United East India Trading Company, with Amsterdam merchants among the major shareholders.

1611   Founding of the Stocks and Commodities Exchange.

1613   The three canals (Herengracht, Keizersgracht and Prinsen-gracht) are built as part of the fourth project to extend the city, with the workers' district of the Jordaan in the W.

1620   The city's population reaches 100,000.

17th c.   The "Golden Age" of Amsterdam, when Amsterdam becomes the most important port in the world.

1780–1784   War with England. Amsterdam loses its supremacy at sea.

19 January 1795   End of the rule of a number of Amsterdam families. Promul-gation of the principles of the French Revolution.

1795–1806   The Low Countries become the Republic of Batavia.

1806   Amsterdam becomes the capital of the Kingdom of the Nether-lands under Louis Napoleon.

1810   The Netherlands are made part of France. The Continental Blockade, which cuts the city off from its traditional markets, finally ends Amsterdam's position as chief trading city.

1813   After the defeat of Napoleon and expulsion of the French, Amsterdam becomes the capital of the Kingdom of the Nether-lands, a constitutional monarchy under William I, although the seat of government is in The Hague.

1839   A railway line is built to Haarlem.

1876   A direct link with the sea is established with the construction of the North Sea Canal. New prosperity for the port.

1913   Social Democrats win a majority on the City Council and Amsterdam is henceforward a stronghold of democratic social-ism.

1914–1918   The Netherlands stay neutral during the First World War. Amsterdam is plunged into a series of crises during this time (unemployment, food shortages, influx of refugees).

1920   Amsterdam has a population of 647,000.

German troops occupy the city. Deportation of Jews is begun.	16 May 1940
The "February Strike" is organised by the workers of Amsterdam in protest against the deportation of their Jewish fellow citizens.	25 February 1941
Although the resistance movement is particularly strong in Amsterdam (underground press, direct action against the forces of occupation), by the end of the war approximately 100,000 Jews have been deported and Amsterdam's Jewish community has been almost completely eliminated.	1940–1945
The city is liberated by Canadian troops.	5 May 1945
Opening of the Amsterdam–Rhine Canal.	1952
Appearance of the anti-Establishment "Provos".	1964–1966
Mass demonstrations triggered off by the wedding of Princess Beatrix and Claus von Amsberg lead to the subsequent dismissal of the Burgomaster and Chief of Police.	10 March 1966
The "Kabouter" (Gnome Party), successors to the Provos, win five seats on the City Council.	1970
Amsterdam celebrates its 700th anniversary; clashes between the residents of the Nieuwmarkt district and the police. Attempts to prevent demolition of housing to make for the Underground.	1975
Over 60,000 on Amsterdam's housing waiting list. Many empty houses occupied by the "Krakers".	1979
Abdication of Queen Juliana. Queen Beatrix pledges her oath of allegiance to the constitution.	30 April 1980
Coronation of Queen Beatrix in the Nieuwe Kerk.	
Riots around the church and palace, away from the heavily protected route of the procession, are directed not so much at the Queen as at the acute housing shortage in Amsterdam.	
Law for the registration of empty dwellings. Illegal occupation of premises prohibited.	1981
Amsterdam applies to stage the Olympic Games in 1992.	1985
Amsterdam celebrates its 400th centenary as a diamond centre. Opening of the new Opera House "Het Musiektheater" on Waterlooplein.	1986
Amsterdam becomes "European City of Culture" for a year, succeeding Athens and Florence in accordance with the 1983 EC Summit decision.	1987
Opening of Amsterdam's new City Hall which shares its building – the "Stopera" – with the "Muziektheater" opera house.	1988

Amsterdam A–Z

*Aalsmeer

Buses
Stop opposite the Central
Station

Location
12 km (8 miles) SW

VVV
Stationsweg 8
Tel. 0 29 77/2 53 74

Open April–Sept., Mon.–Fri.
9 a.m.–5 p.m., Sat.
10 a.m.–noon

The district of Aalsmeer (Province of North Holland) on the canal around the Haarlemmermeer polder is part of the Randstad Holland (see General Information, Randstad Holland). Over one third of its area is covered by lakes, the "Westeinderplassen". It is internationally famous for its flower auctions, which are the largest in Europe.

In the Middle Ages Aalsmeer owed its importance to peat, to fishing and cattle breeding but since about 1450, with the growth of nearby Amsterdam and the 19th c. draining of the Haarlemmermeer, it has become increasingly given over to horticulture.

The flower-growing began with lilac; later the emphasis shifted to pot plants and cut flowers. Today Aalsmeer has over 600 flower-growers, their glass-houses cover an area of 600 hectares (1482 acres) and the annual turnover from the auctions is 380 million guilders.

The flowers are despatched throughout Europe via Schiphol airport (see entry).

There are daily auctions of cut flowers, as well as auctions of pot plants which are held from Monday to Friday between 7.30 and 11 a.m.

Aalsmeer's flower auctions are among the most famous in the world

The auction building has a visitors' gallery where the interested observer can hear a commentary on the auction procedure in any one of seven languages and watch what is going on.
Every year on the first Saturday in September there is a flower parade from Aalsmeer to Amsterdam and back, and this is well worth seeing.

Auctions
Legmeerdijk 313

Achterburgwal (officially: Oudezijds- and Nieuwezijds Achterburgwal) B/C2/3 H/J6

The Nieuwezijds Achterburgwal was dug as a canal in 1380 when the town was being developed and extended from the Spui, the original city boundary, to the Hekelfeld. The canal was filled in in 1867, much to the annoyance of some of the shop-keepers in the Kalverstraat (see entry) who were afraid that the resultant Spuistraat would become a shopping street in com-petition with their own.
Their worries were unfounded because Spuistraat has mainly become a street of offices.

Location
Centre

Metro
Nieuwmarkt

The Oudezijds Achterburgwal was excavated in about 1385 behind the Oudezijds Voorburgwal as a second defensive canal, and stretches from the Grimburgwal to the Zeedijk. It is the narrowest Burgwal and used to be one of the "better" residential areas. Proof of this is the inscription "Fluweelen-burgwal" on the gables of the Driegrachtenhuis (the "House on the three canals" where Grimburgwal, O.Z. Voorburgwal and O.Z. Achterburgwal meet) which alludes to the fact that the prominent citizens of the 17th c. dressed in silk and satin.
House No. 47, among others, is worth seeing. Nowadays the property of the Salvation Army, it used to be the house of the Lieutenant in Rembrandt's painting "The Night Watch".

A little to the SW of the Achterburgwal is the Museum Amstelkring (see entry) which houses a collection of ecclesias-tical antiquities, pictures and copperplate engravings.

Albert Cuypmarkt   H7

The Albert Cuypmarkt has nearly 400 stalls and sells almost everything needed in the kitchen or the home: butter, eggs, cheese, fish, poultry, local and exotic fruits and vegetables, spices, tea, cakes, biscuits, fabrics, wool, haberdashery, pots and pans and cutlery, clothes (new and second-hand), and thousands of odds and ends, some useful, some not. Between van Woustraat and Ferdinand Bolstraat you can stroll at your leisure (although it gets rather crowded on Saturday mornings) and savour the smells of fresh fruit and fish, watch the people around you, listen to the cries of the stall-holders, test the quality of the goods on offer, simply look around or even pick up a bargain.
Those wanting to fortify themselves with coffee and rolls would do well to try the cafe "De Markt" where the stall-holders warm themselves at simple tables in surroundings looking almost the same as when the market first started 75 years ago.

Location
Albert Cuypstraat

Trams
4, 16, 24, 25

Times of opening
Mon.–Sat. 9 a.m.–4.30 p.m.

Alkmaar: famous for its cheese market

*Alkmaar

Rail
From Central Station
(3 times per hour)

Location
37 km (23 miles) NW (A9)

VVV
Waagplein 3
Tel. 0 72/11 42 84

Open in the season
Mon.–Fri. 9 a.m.–5 p.m.,
Sat. 10 a.m.–noon

Alkmaar's number one tourist attraction is its cheese market, held, strictly in accordance with tradition, between 10 and 12 every Friday morning from mid-April to mid-September in front of the weigh-house. The cheese-porters are dressed in white and wear hats bearing the colours of the guild. They carry the cheeses (sometimes 80 Edam cheeses at a time!) on litters, have them weighed on the scales and load them on to carts. (In fact all this is just for show; the actual cheese market is held in the exchange.)

Alkmaar is the ancient centre of North Holland. It lies 8 km (5 miles) from the North Sea coast on the North Holland canal (in the Province of North Holland). Today its major industries are metals, paper, cocoa and carpets.

The town received its charter from Count William II in 1254. In 1517 it fell victim to plundering by a band led by "Big Piet". Alkmaar played a special role in the Dutch struggle for independence from the Spanish by being the first to succeed in routing the son of the Duke of Alba, Frederick of Toledo, who was besieging the town. This took place on 8 October 1573 when the sluices were opened and the surrounding area was flooded.

Alkmaar flourished after the war of independence, owing partly to local land reclamation. Wars of religion raged in the town between 1609 and 1621 but after the lifting of the siege by the French (1810–13), Alkmaar, as an inland town, enjoyed a more peaceful fate than the towns on the Zuiderzee.

Alkmaar's impressive townscape, with its many 16th–18th c.

historic buildings, guild-houses and patrician homes, has been
preserved intact. The finest and most important historic buildings include:
The Grote Kerk (St Laurenskerk, Kerkplein), built 1470–1516, a
late-Gothic cruciform basilica with a famous organ (1645) by
Jacob van Campen.

Times of opening
Mon.–Fri. 9 a.m.–noon,
2–5 p.m.

The Stadhuis (town hall, Langestraat), dating from 1520 with its
late-Gothic front gable.
The weigh-house, converted in 1582 from the former Church of
the Holy Ghost, with a beautiful tower added in 1599. It houses
a cheese museum.

Times of opening
1 Apr.–31 Oct. Mon.–Thurs.
& Sat. 10 a.m.–4 p.m.,
Fri. 9 a.m.–4 p.m.

The Municipal Museum (Stedelijk Museum. Doerenstraat 3),
with its very interesting toy collection. (Admission free)

Times of opening
Mon.–Thurs. 10 a.m.–noon,
2–5 p.m., Fri. 10 a.m.–5 p.m.,
Sun. 2–5 p.m.

Amsterdamse Bos (Amsterdam Wood)   F9/10

The Amsterdam wood was created in 1934 during the Depres-
sion as the result of a "job-creation scheme" which was to
guarantee work for 1000 men for five years. In the 900 ha (over
2000 acres) area on the SW edge of the city can be found about
150 species of trees from all parts of the world, in addition to
shrubs and trees native to the Netherlands. Animal life is just as
varied; more than 200 species of birds find their home here.
The Bos Museum is both an information centre for the leisure
opportunites to be found in the Amsterdamse Bos and at the
same time a museum concerned with the development of the
woodland up to the present day. For children there is a diorama
with stuffed animals.
The wood is very popular with the people of Amsterdam and
offers many sporting facilities, including riding, walking,
cycling, jogging, fishing, swimming, rowing and sailing as well
as restaurants and cafés.
Anyone wishing to stay longer here can make use of the camp
site (see Practical Information, Camp Sites).

Location
Nieuwe Kalfjeslaan
Amstelveen

Museum
Koenenhade

Bus
70

Times of opening
10 a.m.–5 p.m.

---

*Amsterdams Historisch Museum   A3

This museum has been housed in the former municipal
orphanage on the St Luciensteeg since 1975, when Amsterdam
celebrated its 700th anniversary. The name Luciensteeg harks
back to the monastery of St Lucia founded in 1414 which,
besides a chapel and a brewery, also had a farm (today restaurant and museum). After the dissolution of the monastery this
was the municipal orphanage from 1578 to 1960.
Today the restored buildings 1963–1975 surrounding spacious
courtyards are set out as a museum which uses modern methods to illustrate the past. The visitor can learn about the con-
stantly changing position of Amsterdam in the country and in
the world, the growth of the city and the port and the life of its
citizens on its streets and in the home. The exhibits range from
prehistoric finds and the town's original charter, to items from
the present day. Reclamation of the land from the sea is
explained by means of slides. Special exhibitions illustrate
particular aspects of Amsterdam's varied history.

Entrance
Kalverstraat 92

Trams
1, 2, 4, 5, 9, 16, 24, 25

Times of opening
11 a.m. 5 p.m.

Admission fee

Telephone
25 58 22

Amsterdams Historisch Museum

SECOND FLOOR

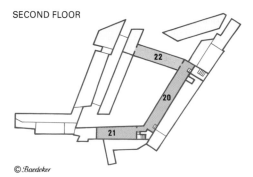

© Baedeker

FIRST FLOOR

© Baedeker

GROUND FLOOR

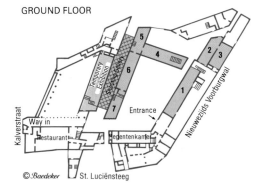

© Baedeker

Kalverstraat
Way in
Restaurant
Regentenkamer
St. Luciënsteeg
Temporary Exhibition
Entrance
Nieuwezijds Voortburgwal

Amsterdams Historisch Museum
in the former municipal orphanage

SECOND FLOOR

20 Handicrafts and trades in the 17th and 18th c.
21 Archaeology
22 Lecture theatre

FIRST FLOOR

8 Work through trade
9 Life in Amsterdam
10 Religious freedom
10 Religious freedom
10A Clock room
11 Rich and poor
12 The 18th c.
13, 14 Development of the arts
15 Science/pleasure
16 "Velvet" revolution
17 Lead-in to the present
18 Copperplate engravings (temporary exhibitions)
19 Library

GROUND FLOOR

1 In the course of time
2 Origins of the city
3 Commerce/pilgrimage
4 Growth and development
5 On the world's seas
6 Powerful city
7 Guns and butter

Historical Museum: entrance and A. J. Vinckenbrinck's "David and Goliath"

There is easy access to the inner courtyards, the shooting gallery, the audio-visual programmes (in English and Dutch) on the history of the building and the restaurant during museum opening hours.

The library possesses a rich collection of literature on the history of the city. In addition graphics, drawings and the Fodor Bequest can be inspected by arrangement. The library is open from Tuesday to Saturday.

Anne Frank Huis (House of Anne Frank)   H5

In this house on the Prinsengracht the Frank family, Jewish refugees from Frankfurt, hid from the Germans with a few friends between 1942 and 1944. Here Anne Frank wrote her famous diary, which has been translated into 51 languages. The final entry is for 1 August 1944. On 4 August they were arrested and sent to concentration camps. Only Anne's father, Otto Frank, survived; Anne herself died in Bergen-Belsen two months before the end of the war.

In 1957 the house was given by its owner to the Anne Frank foundation. The foundation had it restored and turned it into a meeting-place for young people of all nationalities. The front part of the house contains exhibitions of material documenting the persecution of the Jews under the Third Reich and publications on neo-Nazi movements the world over. The back of the house, where the Frank family had their hiding-place, has been kept as far as possible in its original state.

Location
Prinsengracht 263

Buses
21, 67

Trams
13, 17

Times of opening
Mon.–Sat. 9 a.m.–5 p.m.,
7 p.m. in summer, Sun.
and public holidays
10 a.m.–5 p.m.

31

Artis

An Artis enclosure

Artis (officially: Zoo Natura Artis Magistra)   J/K6

Location
Plantage Kerklaan 30–40

Bus
56

Tram
9

Times of opening
9 a.m.–5 p.m.

Admission fee

Amsterdam Zoo was set up by a private association calling itself Natura Artis Magistra (Nature is the instructor of Art), from which the zoo got its name. The aim was to give the townspeople a better understanding of the world of nature by means of exhibits and live animals. In 1838 a site was acquired in the Plantage Middenlaan and the zoo that was built there came to be known as Artis, an abbreviation of the Latin name. There were few animals to start with but their numbers soon grew, for example by purchases from travelling menageries. In its first hundred years the zoo was open only to members of the Association who came here for Sunday walks and attended the concerts held here in the summer months.

When the Association got into financial difficulties the city of Amsterdam and the Province of North Holland bought the zoo and rented it to the Association for the nominal annual sum of one guilder in 1937, since when the zoo has been open to the public.

Right from the start the layout has been continuously extended and modernised. Most animals live in outdoor enclosures corresponding as closely as possible to their natural habitats.

The zoo's main attractions are the aquarium – which, with about 700 species of fish, is the second largest collection in the world (after West Berlin) – and the nocturnal animal house.

Children find the children's farm especially interesting.

The zoo has a very interesting Zoological Museum attached. (See Practical Information, Museums).

Begijnhof: an idyllic spot in the centre of the city

*Begijnhof (Beguine convent)   A3

The Begijnhof is a tiny idyllic spot in the centre of the city where nowadays elderly ladies without families and young women students live for a very low rent. The green lawn of the courtyard is surrounded by houses which include some of the oldest in Amsterdam, among them the only remaining wooden house in the city.

In 1346 the buildings, which at that time still lay outside the city boundaries, were endowed for pious Catholic girls (begijnen) who wanted to live in a religious community but not in the seclusion of a convent. They devoted themselves to the care of the poor and sick. In a "Begijnhof" they were not called upon to abandon their personal freedom and could leave whenever they wished. They had their own accommodation and were not required to renounce personal possessions.

When Amsterdam went over to Protestantism the "begijnen" had to make their church over to the English Presbyterian community and hold their services in secret in a small chapel opposite the church. The Begijnhof was turned into almshouses but the "begijnen" retained the right to be buried in their "old" church. The last "begijn" died in 1971.

Location
Gedempte Begijnensloot
(entrance in Spui)

Trams
1, 2, 4, 16, 24, 25

Bloemenmarkt (Flower market)   A2/3

The flower market on the Singel (see entry) is a Mecca for anyone in search of trees, shrubs, plants, flowers or herbs for the home, garden or balcony. Cut flowers and pot plants of

Location
Singel

Centraal Spoorweg Station

Centraal Station: Amsterdam's central station

Trams
1, 2, 4, 5, 9, 16, 24, 25

Times of opening
Mon.–Sat. 9 a.m.–5 p.m.

every variety, even palms as tall as a man, are offered for sale on the street and on the boats, the whole scene looking like a colourful garden. It is also possible to buy everything imaginable for the garden, such as peat, soil, fertiliser, seeds, tools, watering cans and plant pots.

The flower market has not always been on the Singel; in the 17th c. it was held every Monday in the summer in St Lucien-steeg, near the present-day Historical Museum. It must have had a huge selection to offer then, too, since one contemporary complained that it was difficult and tiresome to list the names of the shrubs and plants on sale.

Centraal Spoorweg Station (Central station)   H/J5 (C1)

Location
De Ruijterkade

Buses
18, 21, 22, 28, 32, 33, 34, 35, 39, 47, 49, 56, 57

Trams
1, 2, 4, 5, 9, 13, 16, 17, 24, 25

Metro
Centraal Station

More than 1000 trains, including 50 international trains, travel in and out of Amsterdam's central station every day. Its architect was P. J. H. Cuypers (also the architect of the Rijksmuseum – see entry) and it was built on three artificial islands and 8687 piles. On the N side of the station (de Ruijterkade), facing the harbour, are the moorings of numerous motor-boats and ferries. The need for the station became apparent when in 1860 Amsterdam was linked to Alkmaar and Den Helder to the N. The public joined in its opening in 1889 with considerable enthusiasm and bought as many as 14,000 platform tickets for the occasion.

The station building, which has an especially interesting Art Nouveau first-class waiting-room, also received international attention, and when in 1900 the Japanese were looking for a model for Tokyo station they opted for Amsterdam.

Concertgebouw   G7

The building of Holland's most famous concert hall was inspired by a German. In 1879 Johannes Brahms was invited to
Amsterdam to conduct his Third Symphony. After the concert
Brahms said: "You are good people but bad musicians!" The
people of Amsterdam took this harsh criticism to heart and
formed a society to establish an orchestra and a concert hall
that would seat about 2000. The concert hall was designed by
A. van Gendt and inaugurated in 1888. The 65-member orchestra was entrusted to Willem Kes who laid the foundations for
the fine reputation both of the orchestra and of the concert hall.
Kes's successor was the 24-year-old Willem Mengelberg who
was associated with the Concertgebouw Orchestra for 50
years. Under his direction it developed into one of the best
orchestras in the world. He introduced the symphonic music of
Mahler and of Richard Strauss who dedicated his "Heldenle-
ben" to Mengelberg. The 1920 Mahler music festival became a
high point in the history of the concert hall. The composers
Reger, Debussy, Ravel, Hindemith, Milhaud and Stravinsky
were guest conductors of their own works in the concert hall.
In the early Eighties, however, there were fears for the future of
this great concert hall when the building, weighing about
10,000 tonnes and underpinned by 2000 posts, threatened to
subside into the muddy subsoil. New foundations were the
saving of the building, which also got a new glass foyer as part
of the renovation works (completed in 1988). The actual concert
hall itself, along with its acoustics, reckoned to be among the
best in the world, remained unaltered.

Location
Van Baerlestraat 98

Telephone
71 83 45

Trams
2, 5, 16

Dam with Nationaal Monument (National Monument)   B2

The Dam, with the Royal Palace (see Koninklijk Paleis) and the
national monument, is no longer either geographically or ad-
ministratively the centre of Amsterdam, but has remained the
heart of the city. It was the Dam which gave the city its name:
built about 1270, it separated the Amstel from the IJ (an arm of
the Zuiderzee – see entry). Amsterdam's history began here
with the founding of the original settlement trading in fish and
cattle. As in the past, the people of Amsterdam still assemble
on the Dam for official events.
In its early days a small market grew up on the square known, in
accordance with medieval custom, as the "Plaetse", and today
the square still retains its market character.

Trams
4, 9, 16, 24, 25

Nationaal Monument (National Monument)

The National Monument, a 22 m (72 ft) high obelisk, was
erected on the Dam after the Second World War. This memorial
to the victims of the war and monument to the Liberation and
peace was designed by J. J. P. Oud and decorated with sculp-
tures by J. W. Rädeler symbolising, among other things, War
(four male figures), Peace (woman and child) and Resistance
(two men with howling dogs).
Embedded in the obelisk are urns containing earth from the
eleven provinces. A twelfth urn contains earth from the cemetery of honour in Indonesia.

Dam with Nationaal Monument

The national monument on the Dam

Delft: some of its famous tiles and an old street organ

The monument was dedicated by Queen Juliana on 4 May 1956, the national day of remembrance, and since then the Dutch Queen and her consort have laid wreaths here every year on that day. A two-minute silence is observed throughout the Netherlands at 8 o'clock that same evening.
The rest of the year the Liberation monument is a place where young people from all over the world meet.

*Delft

Delft, with its picturesque old city centre encircled by canals, is well worth a visit. This town of princes on the River Schie in the Province of South Holland is famous for its blue and white earthenware ("delftware") and for its annual art and antiques fair.

Rail
From Centraal Station

Location
60 km (37 miles) SW (A4, A13)

VVV
Markt 85
Tel. 0 15/12 61 00

Delft received its charter in 1246 and from the 13th c. onwards brewing and carpet-making played important roles. Prince William of Orange (William the Silent) made Delft his seat in 1580. Owing mainly to its earthenware the town reached the peak of its prosperity in the 17th c. when it had 30 tile potteries (1650–1760), but by 1854 only the Royal Delft China Factory "De Porceleyne Fles" remained, and this won a new claim to fame as the manufacturer of Delft-blue china (Rotterdamse Weg 196, can be visited).

A tour of the town should include the following historical buildings:

The Oude Kerk (the Old Church, Oude Delft), which dates from 1250 with subsequent alterations. It has a magnificent pulpit and a number of monumental tombs, the most noteworthy being that of Piet Hein, who captured the Spanish Fleet in 1628.

Open in the season Mon.–Fri. 9 a.m.–5 p.m.,
Sat. 10 a.m.–noon

The Nieuwe Kerk (the New Church, Markt), a Gothic cruciform basilica with a high tower and the burial place of William of Orange. (Organ recitals in the summer.)

Ascent of the tower
Apr.–Sept.: Mon.–Sat.
10 a.m.–noon, 1.30 4 p.m.

The Prinsenhof: originally the Convent of St Agatha, after 1575 it served for a long time as the palace of the Princes of Orange. The Prinsenhof has a tragic place in Dutch history because it was here that William the Silent, the Prince of Orange to whom the country owed its independence, was assassinated in 1584. (Traces still remain at the foot of the steps!)

Times of opening
Tues.–Sat. 10 a.m.–5 p.m.,
Sun. and public holidays
1–5 p.m., June–Aug.: Mon.
1–5 p.m.

Admission fee

The picturesque buildings house the Stedelijk Museum (Oude Delft 185, entrance in St Agathaplein 1), devoted mainly to the 80-year war of Dutch Independence from Spain.

The oldest part of the convent has the only cloister (with double gallery) in the Netherlands.

The Prinsenhof is the venue for the annual antiques fair at the end of October as well as its famous concerts.

The Stadhuis (town hall, Markt 87) has many 16th–18th c. paintings.

Times of opening
Tues.–Sat. 10 a.m.–5 p.m.,
Sun. and public holidays 1–5
p.m.; June–Aug.: 1–5 p.m.

Museum Huis Lambert van Meerten (Oude Delft 199): an important collection of old furniture and paintings and a rich selection of Delftware.

Museum Paul Tétar van Elven (Koornmarkt 67): furnished as an 18th c. mansion and true to its original style.

Times of opening
mid-Apr.–Oct.: Tues.–Sat.
11 a.m.–5 p.m.

Diamond cutting

Amsterdam Diamond Centre

*Diamond cutting

Visits
See Practical Information,
Diamonds

For many people Amsterdam is not only a jewel of a city but also a city of jewels, where diamond cutting and trading have been going on for centuries.

In the middle of the 16th c. many inhabitants of the area which is now Belgium fled to the Netherlands, to escape the Catholic Spaniards for religious reasons. Among the refugees who settled in Amsterdam were many diamond cutters. Thus there arose – to be exact in 1586 – the diamond industry, and in 1986 Amsterdam could celebrate its 400th anniversary as a diamond city. There followed periods of expansion and recession. In about 1750 the industry employed only about 600 people, but the discovery of diamonds in South America (in Brazil in particular) saw an unexpected upturn in its fortunes.

The world's first diamond exhibition was in Amsterdam in 1936.

During the Second World War tens of thousands of Jewish citizens of Amsterdam, including about 2000 diamond-cutters, were deported and never returned.

Today Amsterdam has at least a dozen firms of diamond-cutters and over 60 diamond-processors (see Practical Information, Diamonds).

Only about 20% of diamonds become gemstones (brilliants) for jewellery; the majority are used as industrial diamonds in drills, stone and glass cutters; in boring, grinding and polishing processes and in precision instruments, pick-ups, engraving tools, etc.

Today the trade mark of the diamond-cutters of Amsterdam is still a guarantee of outstanding workmanship and quality.

The largest diamond ever discovered, the famous Cullinan, known as the "Star of Africa", was processed in Amsterdam.

38

Edam town hall

Driegrachtenhuis (House on three canals)

See Achterburgwal

*Edam

The historic little town of Edam in North Holland is in the polder region on the IJsselmeer and is world-famous for its round red-skinned yellow cheeses.

Its people work in industry, agriculture, cattle-breeding and fisheries.

Edam grew up near the dam in the River E which linked the little River Purmer with the Zuiderzee. When, in 1230 the work was begun of damming the rivers flowing into the Zuiderzee (see General Information, Land reclamation, and Amsterdam A–Z: Zuiderzee), merchandise was transported here. Soon customs duties were levied and it became a trading post.

Edam obtained its charter in 1357 and enjoyed its heyday in the 16th–18th c. when shipbuilding, herring fishing and cheese brought economic prosperity to the town. (The warships in which Admiral de Ruyter defeated the English were built in Edam's shipyards.) In 1573 William of Orange granted Edam the right to its own weigh-house for its bravery and services in helping to lift the siege of Alkmaar.

The following buildings in Edam are worth a visit:

The Grote Kerk (or St Nicholas's Church Grote Kerkstraat).

The late-Gothic church has a 15th c. tower and magnificent 17th c. stained-glass windows.

Location
15 km (9 miles) N (E10)

Buses
Stop opposite Centraal Station

VVV
Kleine Kerkstraat 17
Tel. 0 29 93/7 17 27

Open Apr.–Sept. Mon.–Fri. 10 a.m.–12.30 p.m., 1.30–5 p.m., Sat. noon–5 p.m. Oct.–March Mon. –Sat. 10.30 a.m.–noon

The Stadhuis (town hall) dating from 1737 on the Damplein. The registry office still has sand on the floor as it did in the Middle Ages. The council chamber, which is worth seeing in its own right, contains a small exhibition of paintings.

The Stedelijk Museum, Damplein (municipal museum) in a house built in 1540 with an attractive façade dating from 1737 has a floating cellar built in the form of a ship.

The Kaasmarkt (cheese weigh-house) where the original weights can still be seen. Open: Apr.–Sept., daily 10 a.m.–5 p.m. The stretch of water between the two bridges on the Spuistraat is called "Boerenverdriet" ("farmers' dismay"), because the farmers' boats often used to get stuck here.

In July and August boat trips can be made on the Zuiderzee.

Times of opening
Mon.–Sat. 10 a.m.–4.30 p.m.,
Sun. 2–4.30 p.m.

Kassmarkt

Boat trips

Flea market

See Jodenbuurt

*Haven (Port)   E–M 2–6

The port of Amsterdam is 18·5 km (12 miles) from the open sea and, thanks to the IJmuiden sluices, is unaffected by the state of the tide. Several thousand ships call here annually, freighters and also passenger ships. There are regular services up the Rhine to Dusseldorf, Koblenz, Speyer, Strasburg and Basle. In addition Amsterdam is a popular starting point for cruises. Over 37,000 passengers use the port every year.

The port installations were begun in 1872 in conjunction with the construction of the North Sea Canal, the objective being to restore the former importance of the capital city which was being overtaken by Rotterdam. It is well worth joining one of the regular cruises around the harbour and canals, especially in the evening when the houses and bridges are illuminated.

The entire dock area was reclaimed from the IJ. Its channel was deepened and artificial islands with landing quays were built alongside. On the S bank of the IJ there is a series of large wet-docks including the Westerdok, the Oosterdok and the IJhaven, as well as important dockyards.

W of the Westerdok lie the Houthaven (timber), the Minervahaven, the Coenhaven and the spectacular Petroleumhaven, which gives access to the North Sea Canal.

Further W are the Westhaven docks with loading facilities for coal, crude oil, ore and grain, and with oil storage tanks, refineries and chemical plant.

On the N bank of the IJ there are several smaller docks and the locks of the North Holland Canal. Just W of the central station stands the 13-storey Port Administration building, built in 1958–60 by Dudok van Heel, which is 60 m (197 ft) high and has a restaurant with a panoramic view. The Scheepvaartmuseum (see Practical Information, Museum), the Dutch Maritime Museum, is located on the Oosterdok.

Buses
18, 21, 22, 28, 29, 32, 34, 39,
47, 49, 56, 67 (central station)

Trams
1, 2, 4, 5, 9, 13, 16, 17, 24, 25
(central station)

Metro
Centraalstation

Moorings
Steiger (de Ruijterkade)

◄ *The port of Amsterdam: built on land reclaimed from the IJsselmeer*

Impressive both in the past and today: patrician houses on the Herengracht

At the purpose-built Amsterdam Container Terminal container vehicles can be driven straight into the holds of the roll-on roll-off vessels. The opening of the Amsterdam–Rhine Canal in 1952 made for considerably improved links with the European hinterland so far as bulk cargo handling is concerned.

Heineken Brewery   H7

Entrance
v.d. Helstraat 30

Trams
16, 24

Visits
Mon.–Fri. 10–11.30 a.m. with
beer-tasting (free)

The building on the corner of Stadhouderskade and Ferdinand Bolstraat was where Heinekens, one of the Netherlands' biggest breweries, used to brew their beer, but nowadays it only caters for tourists. Heinekens received its licence to brew beer in the mid-19th c. when it also bought up the old-established "Hooiberg" brewery which had been in existence since the Middle Ages when barley brew was the national drink.

Herengracht   H5/6 (A/B1–5)

Location
W and S of the centre

The origins of the Herengracht go back to the year 1612, when a plan to create a girdle of canals (Heren- Keizers- and Prinzengracht) was made. The project was completed in 1658.
In Amsterdam's heyday (second half of 17th c.) the Herengracht was the most elegant residential district. To live here was so popular that the magistrate had to confine the width of the aristocrats' houses to 8 m, but of course there were exceptions, such as the "House for a Prince" (No. 54). Behind the aristocratic houses with their magnificent façades (no fewer

Hoorn town hall (Stadhuis), in a former monastery

than 400 houses in the Herengracht are protected monuments), beautiful gardens were concealed, each of them exactly 51·5 m (169 ft) long. The layout of these gardens represented un-believable luxury for a town which was on piles. A law declared that they could not be built on, an exception, however, was made for summer-houses and coach-houses.

The "golden bocht", the golden arc of the Herengracht, with houses numbered 464–436 (between Vijzelstraat an Leide-straat) is especially noteworthy for its magnificently decorated houses. No. 527 Herengracht, built in 1667, has an interesting history; Tsar Peter the Great of Russia lived here during a visit to Holland. Today the patrician houses are mostly occupied by banks and offices or are used as museum buildings; they have become too large and too expensive to be used as dwellings. Here can be found the Theatrical Museum and the Willet Hol-thuysen Museum (see Practical Information; Museums) and also, at No. 470, the Goethe Institute.

*Hoorn

The town of Hoorn, in the Province of North Holland, the former capital of West Friesland on a bay in the IJsselmeer, is worth a visit. Its main claim to fame is that it used to be an international port, as its many historic buildings testify.

Today Hoorn is an important shopping, leisure, cultural and educational centre and is expected to become more important as a residential town because of its excellent communications with Alkmaar and Amsterdam.

In the 14th c. Hoorn quickly became the market centre of West

Location
40 km (25 miles) N (A8, E10)

Buses
Stop opposite Centraal Station

VVV
See Practical Information, information

Hortus Botanicus

VVV
Statenpoort, Nieuwstraat 23
Tel. 02290/18342

Friesland and received its charter in 1356. In the second half of that century Hoorn already overshadowed the older towns of the Zuiderzee, Enkhuizen and Medemblik, and in the 16th c. the town became the major international port on the Zuiderzee. By the middle of the 17th c., however, Hoorn was already starting to decline in economic importance.

Hoorn numbers among its famous men Willem Schouten who sailed round the southern tip of America in 1616 and named it "Kap Hoorn" (Cape Horn) after his home town; Count Philip van Hoorn, a Knight of the Order of the Golden Fleece, who, together with Count Egmont, was executed in Brussels on 5 June 1568 for his part in the Dutch Wars of Independence against Spain; and Jan Pieterszoon, Coen, Governor of the Dutch East Indies and founder of Batavia (now Djakarta, Indonesia).

Places worth visiting in Hoorn include:

Noorderkerk

The Noorderkerk, in Kleine Noord (North Church; built in 1426, restored in 1938), a hall basilica (with three naves of equal height), a late-Gothic spiral staircase and sumptuous Renaissance furnishings. The church is open to visitors during exhibitions.

Oosterkerk

The Oosterkerk, in Groote Oost (East Church; built 1450), a single-nave cruciform church with a Renaissance façade (1616). Its interior dates from the early 17th c. and the organ from 1765. For times of opening enquire at VVV.

Stadhuis

The former Stadhuis (town hall, 1613; Nieuwstraat 23). Since the town hall moved to a new location, this building has been occupied by the Tourist Office.

St Peterhof

The St Peterhof (1692), now an old people's home with a picturesque 17th and 18th c. interior.

Three 16th c. towers (inc. Oosterpoort).

Westfries Museum
Times of opening
Mon.–Fri. 11 a.m.–5 p.m., Sat., Sun. and public holidays 2–5 p.m.

A visit to the West Friesian Museum (Westfries Museum, Rodesteen 1), is highly recommended. It has collections of old paintings, porcelain, costumes and toys and in the cellar there is an archaeological department.

Old Dutch Market

An old Dutch market (Rodesteen) is held every Wednesday in July and August where ancient handicrafts are demonstrated by local people in period costume.

Hortus Botanicus (Botanical garden of the Municipal University)   D4 (J6)

Location
Plantage Middenlaan 2

Tram
9

Times of opening
Mon.–Fri. 9 a.m.–4 p.m.; Sat,. Sun. and public holidays 11 a.m.–4 p.m.

The botanical garden of the municipal university, with its exotic flowers, trees and plants, dates back to the time of the monastery herb gardens. The Vlooienburg botanical garden (with some 2000 native trees, plants, herbs and shrubs) came into existence in 1554 with the publication of a book about plants which described not only the plants themselves but also their healing properties. The garden was frequently relocated and enlarged and in 1877 became the property of the university. The Vrije University also maintains a botanical garden (see Practical Information, Parks). Admission fee.

IJ tunnel   J5

Over 100 years ago people were looking at ways of linking Amsterdam with the opposite bank of the IJ in the N (link with

Jewish Historical Museum

North Holland). A tunnel was being thought of even at that time (plans for a suspension bridge are even older), since the ferries to and from North Holland caused considerable delays. For a long time, however, such plans were thought unrealistic, and it was not until the beginning of this century that the city council was prepared seriously to examine the idea of a tunnel. From 1930 to 1950 countless designs were discussed and rejected but it was finally decided to build a tunnel for road vehicles only. Cyclists and pedestrians still have to use the ferries. On 25 May 1955 the first pile was driven into the ground but the project was dogged by organisational and financial problems and it was years before the work was completed at a total cost of over 20 million guilders. In October 1968 the tunnel was opened to traffic and brought great improvements in communications with North Holland.

Jodenbuurt (Jewish quarter)　　　　　J6 (C/D 3/4)

The former Jewish quarter extends from the Houtkoopersburg-wal in the N to the Binnen-Amstel in the S. The first Jewish refugees came to Amsterdam at the end of the 16th c. and settled in the area around the Waterlooplein (Jodenbreestraat, Valkenburgerstraat, Oude Schans). They were mostly from Portugal (see Portuguese synagogue), but also from Germany and Poland. The Jewish quarter had a special charm, with its countless little second-hand shops, haberdashers and green-grocers.

A market used to be held on the Waterlooplein on Sundays, although it was hard to see how the dealers could make a living

Location
Around the Waterlooplein

Tram
9

Metro
Waterlooplein

from selling their second-hand goods. After the Second World War hardly anything was left of what had once been the charming Jewish quarter around the Waterlooplein. Deportation robbed the streets of their people – of the 140,000 Jews who lived in Amsterdam before the War only a fifth survived the Holocaust.

In the Sixties the building of an expressway drastically changed the face of the quarter, then a cutting was made for the building of the Metro, leaving only a row of houses on the Amstel, until those too were demolished in 1976.

The Waterlooplein has made a comeback, however. Today it is the site of Amsterdam's opera house, "Het Muziektheater", which shares its building with the new town hall (see Stopera), and the Jewish past is recalled in the Joods Historisch Museum (see entry).

*Vlooienmarkt

Market times
Mon.–Sat.10 a.m.–5 p.m.

After almost a ten-year interval Amsterdam's famous flea-market, the Vlooienmarkt, is back on the Waterlooplein where it had been held since 1886.

"Whether there are fleas in the flea market in Amsterdam is hard to say; there is certainly everything else. Threadbare clothes, once the height of fashion, and factory surplus lie side by side waiting for buyers, to be gaped at, smiled at, scoffed at, unsold."

This is one writer's description of the scene on the Waterlooplein, where dealers large and small offer their wares for sale on stalls or simply on the ground - a colourful jumble of junk and handy bits and pieces, a tatty treasure trove. Although new goods are on sale as well the emphasis is still on old second-hand goods.

---

*Joods Historisch Museum (Jewish Historical Museum)   D4 (J6)

Location
Jonas D.Meijerplein 2–4

Tram
9

Metro
Waterlooplein

Opening times
11 a.m.–5 p.m.

In 1987 the Jewish Historical Museum moved into its new premises - four redundant synagogues right next to the Waterlooplein.

The first of the four synagogues, the Grote Synagoge, or Grote Sjoel, was built in 1670 but soon after its consecration was already proving too small. In 1686, therefore, a second, smaller synagogue, the Obbene Sjoel, was built behind the Great Synagogue and over the kosher slaughterhouse. The third synagogue, the Dritt Sjoel, was added in 1700 and finally, in 1752, the new synagogue, the Neie Sjoel, completed the complex. This was sold in its entirety to the City of Amsterdam by the Jewish Community in 1955. In the mid-Seventies the city decided that it should be put to a new use. The buildings were restored for a budget of over £8 million, and joined together using steel and glass to create a very attractive, highly accessible building that now houses what is probably the most important Jewish museum outside Israel.

New Synagogue

The tour of the museum complex begins in the New Synagogue where the visitor is introduced to "Aspects of the Jewish identity". Here the five crucial elements are seen as being religion, Zionism, persecution and survival under the Nazis, culture, and the influence of the Dutch environment. The Great Synagogue houses the ritual objects in the collection – silver

Great Synagogue

Torah containers, Torah robes and decorated Torah head-
dresses, hangings and baldaquins – and on the eastern wall of
the synagogue, pointing towards Jerusalem, the white marble
"Holy Shrine".
The permanent exhibits are supplemented by temporary exhibitions. The museum also has a mediatheque full of books,
tapes, and audio-visual material, and in the Upper Synagogue,
the Obbene Sjoel, there is a kosher restaurant.

In the square in front of the Jewish Historical Museum there is
the statue of "the Docker". This is a monument commemorating the dockers' strike in February 1941 when they refused to
co-operate with the deportation of their Jewish fellow citizens.

Docker Monument

Jordaan

G5–6/H5

To the W of the city centre, between Prinsengracht (see entry)
and Lijnbaansgracht, lies the Jordaan, the working-class dis
trict made famous by the many songs about it. It came into
being when the city was extended in the early 17th c. and many
small craftsmen set up shop here. Refugees settled in the quarter during the Thirty Years War and artists (including Rembrandt) were so attracted by the Jordaan that they made their
homes here.
There are many theories about the name "Jordaan". The most
likely is that it comes from the French word "jardin", meaning
"garden", but whether or not the quarter owes its name to its
many little front gardens and backyards there were certainly
many Walloons and French living here when the Jordaan got
its name.
Life in the Jordaan is still largely lived out on the streets.
Originally this was for practical reasons (large families, small
houses) but nowadays it is on grounds of sociability. The Jordaan still has its own special atmosphere, with convivial corner
pubs, sweet-shops kept by little old ladies and tiny boutiques.
Artists and eccentrics are consequently irresistibly drawn to
this quarter, where many long-established Amsterdamers can
still be encountered.

Location
Between Prinsengracht and
Lijnbaansgracht

Trams
3, 10, 13, 17

*Kalverstraat

A/B2–4 (H6)

The Kalverstraat is the meeting place for half Amsterdam. Its
smart boutiques and perfumeries make it the city's best-known
shopping street, although the P.C.Hooftstraat has overtaken it
as "the" top address.
First mentioned in 1393 it gets its name from the calf-trade.
There is no proof that cattle-markets were actually held in this
street, but cattle were certainly driven through the Kalverstraat
to the calf-market which in the 16th c. took place on the Dam.
Needless to say, the first businesses to settle in the Kalverstraat
were the butchers, later followed by craftsmen, including cob-
blers and basket-makers. In the mid-18th c. there were already
more than 200 shops of all kinds here, as well as coffee-shops
and boarding houses.
Nowadays the Kalverstraat is a pedestrian precinct and attracts
up to 100,000 shoppers a day. On Saturdays the crush is fright-
ening. It can take at least half an hour to walk from the Munt to

Location
Between Dam and Muntplein

Trams
1, 2, 4, 5, 9, 16, 24, 25

the Dam instead of the usual 10 minutes – that is if you manage to get there at all and are not swept along by the crowd in quite a different direction.

The only Madame Tussaud's outside London was opened in 1970 at 156 Kalverstraat. Besides contemporary personalities such as Queen Beatrix, Margaret Thatcher and François Mitterand, there are also historic wax figures like Napoleon and Peter the Great. A whole room is given over to Rembrandt, and in another it is possible to stroll round Hieronymus Bosch's Garden of Delights. The workroom where the wax figures are made is also on view.

Madame Tussaud's
Panopticum

The Panopticum is open daily from 10 a.m. to 6 p.m., and till 7 p.m. in July and August.

Keizersgracht   H/J5/6 (A–C1/2/3/4)

The middle one of the three canals does not quite come up to the elegant standards of the Herengracht (see entry).

Location
W of Centraal Station to S of Rembrandtsplein

The finest houses are to be found between the Westermarkt and Vijzelstraat. This part was also famed in the last century for the "slipper parade" which took place here on Sundays after church when, between 2 and 4 in the afternoon, most of Amsterdam strolled up and down here in their Sunday best in order to see and be seen.

Famous houses on the Keizersgracht include:

The House with the Golden Chain (No. 268): an old mansion out of which hangs a golden chain. There are many legends purporting to explain the significance of this chain. According to one tale, a maid was accused of stealing a golden chain from her mistress but the chain was discovered in a crow's nest so the maid was reinstated.

Another story tells of a captain who lived in the house and had grown weary of going to sea. When forced to go to sea again for financial reasons, he swore to bring back a golden chain if fortune smiled on him or an iron chain if she did not. Obviously fortune smiled, hence the golden chain.

There are other traditional legends, but the true story seems to be that it was the home of a goldsmith and the golden chain, which has hung in front of the house since 1643, served as his trademark.

The House with the Heads (No. 123) dates from 1622 and is one of the finest mansions in the city. The gable is decorated with six helmeted heads, but there is also supposed to be a seventh female head. The story goes that it was the home of a rich merchant who had a deaf maid. One day when the maid was alone in the house thieves broke in but were all beheaded by the maid.

Today it houses offices.

The Fodor Museum is at number 609 and open daily from 11 a.m. to 5 p.m. It shows the work of contemporary artists, preferably those actually living in Amsterdam. When it was first opened in 1863 the Museum housed the collection of a coal merchant by the name of C. J. Fodor, which can nowadays be found in the Amsterdams Historisch Museum (see entry).

Fodor Museum

The building at number 672 which today holds the Van Loon

Van Loon Museum

◀ *Keizergracht: a reminder of Amsterdam's venerable past*

Keukenhof

Keukenhof: Holland's flower paradise

Times of opening
Mondays only, 10 a.m.–5 p.m.

Museum is also particularly worth seeing. It was built for a Flemish merchant in 1672 and became the property of the Van Loons in 1884. The interior is furnished in typical mid-18th century style and besides various art objects includes a gallery of over 50 family portraits from the 17th and 18th c. The Museum also has a lovely formal rococo garden.

*Keukenhof

Location
Lisse, 35 km (20 miles) SW

Rail
From Centraal Station to Haarlem and Leiden

Times of opening
end of Mar. to end of May:
daily 8 a.m.–7.30 p.m.

The Keukenhof, in the heart of the Dutch flower-growing area between Haarlem and Leiden (see entry), has since 1949 been a special place for an excursion: the National Flower Exhibition takes place here every year from the end of March to the end of May on a 28 hectare (69 acre) site.

Apart from every imaginable type of bulb the Keukenhof also has shrubs such as rhododendrons and azaleas. Even before the flowers in the grounds are in bloom, hundreds of thousands of crocuses, hyacinths, narcissi and, above all, tulips can be admired in huge greenhouses (5000 sq. m/53,820 sq. feet) from 9 in the morning until sunset. In the Juliana Pavilion and the Konigin Beatrix Pavilion exhibitions and other events are held.

From the second half of April until the beginning of May the five million flowers in the grounds of the Keukenhof are at the height of their splendour and there is a magnificent view of it all from a windmill. The nearby 19th c. castle is also worth seeing.

The impressive Koninklijk Paleis on the Dam ▶

Koninklijk Paleis (Royal palace) A2

Trams
1, 2, 4, 5, 9, 13, 16, 17, 24, 25

Buses
21, 67

Open during the summer
Mon.–Sat. 12.30–4 p.m.; at
other times guided tours on
Wed. at 2 p.m.

Admission free

The Royal Palace on the Dam (see entry), formerly the town hall, constitutes an impressive central point of Amsterdam. Nowadays it serves as the Queen's residence when she is in the city.

Building began on 20 January 1648 with the sinking of the first of 13,659 piles for the new town hall. Its architect was Jacob van Campen whose inspiration was the architecture of Ancient Rome; the exterior is strictly classical and the interior is magnificently furnished. The apartments are decorated with a wealth of reliefs, ornamentation and marble sculpture by the Flemish sculptors Artus Quellinus and Rombout Verhulst, and with friezes and ceiling-paintings by Ferdinand Bol and Govert Flinck, pupils of Rembrandt.

Van Campen was, however, unable to finish the building and Stalpaert took over from him in 1654. Costs had risen so much in the meantime that work on the tower of the New Church (see Nieuwe Kerk) had to be suspended. The new town hall with the 51 m (167 ft) high tower (carillon) was finally completed in 1665. For about 200 years this imposing building, the greatest work of the 17th c. Dutch Classicism, was the political centre of Amsterdam and the republic. In 1808, however, Louis Napoleon, Holland's new king, wanted it for his own residence. His Empire furniture from that time is still one of the finest collections in the world. With the ending of Napoleonic rule the town hall reverted to the city which, however, because of its financial straits, was unable to use it for its original purpose and let it to King William I as a temporary residence. In 1935 the State bought the palace for 10 million guilders and had it extensively restored for use on official occasions.

The finest rooms, and the most interesting from the art historian's point of view, are those overlooking the Dam. The city treasurer's room has an interesting marble fireplace and ceiling paintings by Cornelius Holsteyn. The Hall of the Aldermen contains paintings by Ferdinand Bol and Govert Flinck and a work by Jan Lievens hangs in the Mayor's Chamber.

The largest and most important room is the Council Hall (34×13×16·75 m (112×13×55 ft) and 28 m (92 ft) high). This sumptuously decorated hall (one of the most beautiful state rooms in Europe) was where the ball celebrating the marriage of the Crown Princess Beatrix to Claus von Amsberg was held in 1966.

Mention should also be made of the ante-room (Vierschaar) which contains four outstanding caryatids (figures supporting beams) by A. Quellinus the Elder.

*Leiden

Location
40 km (25 miles) SW

Rail
From Centraal Station
via Schiphol

The old university town of Leiden (or Leyden) in the Province of South Holland lies on the sluggish Old Rhine which flows like a canal through the town. For many centuries it was an industrial town, and was known in the Middle Ages for its cloth-weaving. Nowadays its major industries are machinery and printing (its far-eastern prints are world-famous). Leiden has several

The university building: the chapel of a former monastery

historic buildings, a great many museums and the largest indoor cattle market in the Netherlands.

In the 12th c. the Counts of Holland built first a castle then a palace (where Floris V was born) on a rise overlooking the Old Rhine. The little town of Leiden grew up between the castle and the palace and received its charter in 1266. In the 14th c. the town was the centre of the cloth industry. On 3 October 1574 William of Orange freed Leiden from the Spanish siege which, accompanied by plague and starvation, had lasted almost a year, and this event is still annually celebrated.

In 1575 the town was rewarded for its bravery with a university which later became an important European centre of culture.

Several important artists and scholars were born here in the 17th c. including Rembrandt van Rijn (1606–69), Jan Steen (1626–79), Gerard Dou (1613–75) and Herman Boerhave (1668–1738).

The following places are worth a visit:

The imposing castle was built in 1150 on an artificial mound, about 12 m/39 ft high, at the confluence of the Old and the New Rhine as a refuge from flooding. The castle courtyard inside the encircling wall and battlements is about 35 m/115 ft across. Located at 14 Burgsteeg, the Burcht is open Mon.–Sat. 8 a.m.–11 p.m. and Sun. 11 a.m.–11 p.m.

Prior to 1581 the old University building on the Rapenburg was the chapel of a Dominican monastery.

The 17th c. town hall on the Breestraat, which has a carillon, had a magnificent Renaissance façade which was almost

VVV
210 Stationsplein
Tel. 0 71/14 68 46

Open in the season
Mon.–Fri. 9 a.m.–5 p.m.,
Sat. 10 a.m.–noon

Burcht

Universiteit

Stadhuis

totally destroyed by fire in 1929. It has been partly restored in the old style.

Pieterskerk

St Peter's Church in the Pieterskerkhof dates from around 1315. It is a late Gothic basilica (the tower collapsed in 1512 and was never rebuilt), with an impressive pulpit and various tombs. These include the tomb of John Robinson who in Leiden founded in 1611 the first congregation of Independents (Puritans who had been driven out of England).

Gravensteen

The Gravensteen, with its classical façade, was originally a prison for the counts and then for the town. It now forms part of the Law Faculty of the University.

Stedelijk Museum

The municipal museum, which is at 28–32 Oude Singel, and open Tues.–Sat. 10 a.m.–5 p.m. and Sundays and public holidays 1–5 p.m., is in the Lakenhal (Cloth Hall, 1639) which formerly housed the Guild of the cloth-weavers. Besides important 17th–18th c. works by artists such as Corm, Lucas van Leyden, Rembrandt and Jan Steen, it also has an exhibition relating the history of weaving.

Rijksmuseum van Oudheden

The national archaeological museum at 28 Rapenburg (open Jan.–Sep. Tues.–Sat. 10 a.m.–5 p.m., Sundays and public holidays 1–5 p.m.) has a large collection of Greek, Etruscan and Roman sculpture, ancient vases and artefacts, as well as archaeological finds, mostly from the Netherlands.

Botanical Gardens

The Botanical Gardens are at 73 Rapenburg (open May–Sep. Mon.–Fri. 8.30 a.m.–5.30 p.m., Sundays and public holidays 2–5 p.m.). They date from 1587 and also have a planetarium.

Leidseplein   G6

Trams
1, 2, 5, 6, 7, 10

Amsterdam's second-largest amusement and entertainment centre (after the Rembrandtplein) caters for all tastes with two theatres (the Municipal Theatre and De Balie, formerly a prison), countless cinemas, hotels and restaurants in every price-category, night clubs, bars, cabarets and pubs. From Shakespeare to striptease, it's all there on the Leidseplein which pulsates with life until well into the night.
The lively atmosphere of the Leidseplein is not a modern phenomenon. It was here that the farmers used to leave their carts and have their horses looked after when they came into town for the market. Today the square's cosmopolitan atmosphere comes from the Stadschouwburg (Municipal Theatre – see entry), the Hotel Américain and pavement cafés (including the Café Reynders, a meeting-place for artists and journalists) and, last but not least, the many visitors both from home and abroad.

Lieverdje   A3

Location
Spui

Trams
1, 2, 5

The Lieverdje on the Spui (an Amsterdam street-urchin) was originally a plaster figure made by the sculptor Carel Kneulman for a local festival. A manufacturer found the lad so appealing that he had it cast in bronze and presented it to the city.

Magere Brug: the most photographed of all Amsterdam's bridges

It was unveiled on the Spui on 10 September 1960 and has since proved a favourite rallying point for political action because of its central position near the university, and as an anti Establishment symbol.
In the mid-sixties it was here that the "Provos", the spontaneous young people's movement of that time, mounted 'happenings' and handed out their first manifestos.

Magere Brug (Mager bridge) C4

Of Amsterdam's 1000 or so bridges the "Magere Brug" near the Weesperstraat is the most photographed.
This simple wooden drawbridge over the Amstel was built in 1671 as a footbridge. After being renovated several times it was demolished in 1929. It was to be replaced by a modern electrically operated bridge but it was finally decided to build a wooden reconstruction of the original.
The building work was supervised by the architect Mager who gave his name to the bridge.

Location
Amstel/Nieuwe Kerkstraat

Trams
4

Metro
Weesperplein

Marken

Marken used to be an island in the IJsselmeer but since 1957 it has been linked to the Nes headland by a 2 km (1¼ miles) long

Location
22 km (14 miles) NE

Marken

Marken: dancing on the ice

Rail
From Centraal Station

Bus
From opposite Centraal Station

VVV
See Practical Information, Information: Monnickendam

dyke. This dyke is one of the ring of dykes that will encircle the Markerwaard polder which is to be the fourth area reclaimed from the Zuiderzee (see Zuiderzee and General Information, Land Reclamation).

Since fishing lost its importance with the damming of the Zuiderzee, tourism has become the main source of income for the peninsula and 80% of Marken's population work outside the area.

In 1232 Marken was a monastic settlement attached to the Friesian abbey of Mariengaard which owned the whole island from 1251 to 1345 when it was bought by the city of Amsterdam. This meant that in the Middle Ages it was often the scene of the quarrels that determined the relationship between Amsterdam and the ports on the opposite bank of the Zuiderzee (e.g. Kampen). In the 17th c. shipping flourished here, and Marken became independent during the French occupation (c. 1811). By the late 19th c. Marken had 17 residential districts, but today there are only seven villages in addition to the main village of Monnikenwerf.

The principal attraction for tourists in Marken are the architecture of its houses – until 1931 the wooden houses were built on piles – and the folk costumes which are still worn there.

The women wear a "ryglyf", a type of semi-transparent bodice that is either dark blue or embroidered with various colours.

The island is still very Calvinist, so one should not expect to be invited to a winter wedding which is best celebrated on the frozen Zuiderzee – in the traditional costumes, of course, with music and folk dancing, the women dancing together.

The people of Marken still hold an Easter procession.

Mozes-en-Aaronkerk: once a "secret" Catholic church, now a youth centre ▶

Times of opening
Easter–Oct.: Mon.–Sat.
10 a.m.–4.30 p.m.,
Sun. noon–4 p.m.

In the local museum of Marken (Marker Museum, Kerbuurt 44–47) the visitor can see a vivid representation of everyday life of the inhabitants of the former island.

Monnickendam

Location
13 km (8 miles) NE

Buses
Stop opposite Centraal Station

Motorboat
From Stationsplein or de Ruijterkade (summer only)

VVV
2 Zarken
Tel.0 29 95/19 98
(open April–Sep.: Mon.–Sat.
10a.m.–7p.m.; Oct.–March:
Mon.–Sat. 10a.m.–12.30p.m.)

Times of opening
Mid-June to mid-Aug.: 10.30
a.m.–12.30 p.m.,
2–4 p.m., Sun. 2–4.30 p.m.

Times of opening
By appointment:
tel. 02995/3939

Monnickendam is a small old town in North Holland on the banks of the Gouwzee and the IJsselmeer and its location explains why it is best known for its smoked fish and as a centre for water sports.

About 70% of Monnickendam's working population have jobs elsewhere and the rest are in business and tourism.

Monnickendam was founded by monks in the 12th c. and was granted its charter in 1335. Its position on the Zuiderzee (see entry) with its busy shipping trade soon brought it fame and prosperity but by the 17th c. only fishing remained as an important source of income, and life in Monnickendam had adjusted accordingly. Various catastrophes also struck the town: in 1297 it was raided by the Friesians and in 1494 and 1514 large sections of the town were destroyed by fire.

Some of the places of interest:

The Belfry (Speeltoren, in Noordeinde) dating from the 16th c. with its 18-bell carillon (1596).

The Groote Kerk (or St Nicholas's Church, in Zarken, built in 1400) which houses a collection of tiles and majolica ware.

The Stadhuis (town hall), at Noordeinde 5, originally built as a private mansion in 1746, has a council chamber with golden wallpaper and a Rococo ceiling.

Be sure to visit the "Haringhallen" eel-smoking establishments (Palingrokerejen).

From Monnickendam boat trips can be made to Marken and Volendam between April and September daily from 9 a.m. –4.45 p.m.

*Mozes-en-Aaronkerk (Moses and Aaron Church)   C3

Location
Jodenbreestraat

Metro
Waterlooplein

Tram
9

The history of this church goes back to the "Alteratie" (see General Information, History of the City) when secret churches sprang up everywhere, since Catholics no longer dared to hold services in public. In 1641 Father Boelenzs purchased the Moses and Aaron House in Jodenbreestraat from a rich Jew and converted it into a church. In the course of time the church was enlarged, and it was consecrated in 1841, after its transformation into its present neo-Classical form by a Belgian architect.

Today the Moses and Aaron Church is no longer a house of God but a youth club where yoga is taught, tea dispensed and sitar concerts given. There are still times, however, when foreign workers threatened with deportation come here in search of a secret refuge.

Muntplein with Munttoren (Mint tower)   B4 (H6)

Location
Southern centre

The main shopping streets, Rokin, Kalverstraat (see entry) and Reguliersbreestraat, start from the Muntplein.

In the 15th c. this square on the Amstel next to the city wall, known at the time as Sheep Square, was where the sheep market was held. Its present name dates from 1672 when money was coined in the Mint (the former guardroom next to the Mint tower).

Trams
4, 9, 16, 24, 25

Munttoren (Mint tower)

The name "Mint tower" dates from 1672 when, for two years, Amsterdam was the site of the mint while the French occupied Utrecht where coins were usually minted. The Munttoren is part of the medieval city walls which were almost completely destroyed in the great fire of 1818. The lower part of the tower was left standing. On the remaining stones the city architect Henrick de Keyser placed a wooden structure (with a carillon by Hemony) and a gilded weather-vane in the shape of an ox, as a reminder of the calf-market which had been held on the nearby Dam (see entry). When this weather-vane fell from the top of the tower during a storm in 1840 it was replaced by the usual weather-cock.

Museum Amstelkring   C2

The museum, with a "secret" Catholic church, is nicknamed "Ons' Lieve Heer op Zolder" ("Our dear Lord in the Attic"). After the Reformation, when the Catholics had to hold their services in secret, a secret oratory for around 200 believers was set up under the roof of this private house. If danger threatened there was a way out through the skylight.
After the death of its Catholic owner the house fell into the hands of non Catholics, but services still took place here until 1888.
Later the Amstelkring foundation turned the house and church into a museum in which the atmosphere of the 17th c. "secret church" can still be experienced today. Besides the original oratory (with organ and altar), private 18th c. chambers housing a collection of church antiquities, pictures and engravings are also open to visitors.
The museum still functions as a church. Concerts of Baroque music are also held here in the winter months.

Location
Oudezijds Voorburgwal 40

Trams
4, 9, 16, 24, 25

Times of opening
Mon.–Sat. 10 a.m.–5 p.m.;
Sun. and public holidays
1–5 p.m.

*Nieuwe Kerk (New Church)   A/B2

Location
Dam

Trams
1, 2, 4, 5, 9, 13, 16, 17, 24, 25

Times of opening
Mon.–Sat. 11 a.m.–4 p.m.,
Sun. noon–5 p.m.

Closed
Jan. and Feb.

The Coronation church of the Dutch monarchs (since 1814) lies in the heart of the city next to the Royal Palace (see Koninklijk Paleis) on the Dam (see entry), and its most recent great event (after 22 years of renovation work) was the coronation of Queen Beatrix on 30 April 1980.
The church is no longer used for services. Antique fairs, art exhibitions and regular organ concerts take place here.
Strangely enough this church has only a small tower instead of a high steeple. The money for something larger was not forthcoming because it had been used to build the Royal Palace.
The church dates from the early 15th c. Its foundation charter is dated 1408 when the Bishop of Utrecht granted the city of Amsterdam the right to have a second parish (the first was that

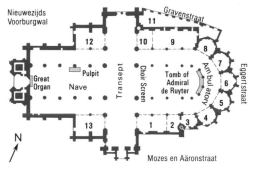

Nieuwezijds
Voorburgwal

Gravenstraat

11

12 10 9

8

7

Great
Organ Pulpit

Nave Transept Choir Screen Tomb of
Admiral
de Ruyter Ambulatory Eggertstraat

6

5

13 1 2 3

4

N

Mozes en Aäronstraat

Nieuwe Kerk
St Catherine

1 Sanctuary
2 Eggert Chapel
3 Chapel of Our Lady of the Seven
   Sorrows (Sills Chapel)
4 Chapel of concealment
5 Meeus Chapel
6 Bricklayers' Chapel
7 Boelens Chapel
8 Cloth-workers' Chapel
9 Crucifix Chapel
10 Chapel of Our Lady
11 Deaconry
12 Old Crucifix Choir
13 Headmaster's house

of the Oude Kerk – see entry).

The Amsterdam banker William Eggert presented the site.
After his death he was buried in the church and his son had a
chapel named after him built on to the church.

When Amsterdam was ravaged by fire in 1421 and 1452 the
New Church suffered considerable damage, but in each case
was quickly restored. Its present aspect dates roughly from
1490.

The imposing late-Gothic cruciform basilica was almost completely burnt down in 1645 owing, it is said, to the carelessness
of a craftsman. After its reconstruction, which took about three
years, the church was reconsecrated with a service of thanks-
giving for the Peace of Münster (1648).

The magnificent pulpit (1649) by Albert Vinckenbrink, a marvel
of Baroque woodcarving, is decorated with the four evangelists
and figures symbolising Faith, Hope, Charity, Justice and Pru-
dence. The church has a notable organ of 1670, the case of
which was designed by Jacob van Campen, an exceptionally
beautiful choir screen, cast in bronze, and fine choir-stalls.

Of great interest are the tombs of many famous Dutchmen,
including P. C. Hooft and Nicholas Tulp and the Baroque tomb
of Admiral Michiel de Ruyter (d. 1679) by the high altar.

The stained-glass windows are also interesting: one of them
(dated 1650) depicts the granting of the city's coat of arms by
Willam IV; the Queen's Window (1898) commemorates the
coronation of Queen Wilhelmina.

Nieuwmarkt   C2/3

Location
Nieuwmarkt

Metro
Nieuwmarkt

There actually used to be a market on the Nieuwmarkt in the
17th and 18th c. and it was divided up into individual plots for
the stalls selling cheese, fish, herbs and cloth.

During the Second World War the Nieuwmarkt was widely
known for its flourishing Black Market.

In 1975 there were street riots in this area when the local people
gave vent to their anger at the demolition of many houses for
the construction of the Underground.

The Nieuwmarkt is the site of the Waaggebouw (see entry),
built as a gateway to the city in 1488.

Oude Kerk
St Nicolaas

1 South Portal (entrance)
2 Iron Chapel
3 Smiths' Chapel
4 St Sebastian's Chapel
5 Seamen's Chapel
6 Remains of the former Chapel of the Holy Tomb
7 Chamber of the Guild of Our Lady
8 Old Female Choir
9 New Female Choir (stained glass)
10 Tomb of St Joris
11 Holy Tomb
12 Buckwheat Merchants' Chapel
13 Old North Portal (c. 1520)
14 Shippers' Chapel
15 Hamburg Chapel
16 Former Baptistery (c. 1462)
17 Lijsbeth Gaven Chapel
18 Chapel of the Poor

Oudekerksplein

Olympisch Stadion (Olympic Stadium)   E/F8

Amsterdam's most important sports centre is the Olympic Stadium. Built in 1928 when the Olympic Games were held in the Netherlands, it originally held 40,000 spectators but after being extended in 1936 it now holds 60,000. Athletic and speedway meetings and cycle races take place in the stadium.

Location
Stadionplein

Trams
6, 16, 24

*Oude Kerk (Old Church)   B/C2

Amsterdam's oldest church was built in 1306 as a small cruciform church to replace a wooden church which is thought to have been built here in about 1300. It was the first hall church (i.e. with the aisles the same height as the nave) in North Holland and the model for other churches in the region (e.g. in Edam). It was dedicated to St Nicolaas by the Bishop of Utrecht. There were soon plans for enlarging it and in 1370 two chapels were built on to the choir and an ambulatory added. The church was spared the two great fires which devastated Amsterdam in the Middle Ages. Other chapels were partly endowed by guilds. The large side chapels were added around 1500. The alterations to the choir in the 16th c. were financed (as was usual in those days) by a lottery. Also dating from this period is a portal on the S side which gives access to the "iron" chapel, where the documents showing the city's privileges, including the freedom from tolls granted in 1275, were kept behind an iron door, until they were finally transferred to the municipal archives in 1872.

The tower was also remodelled in the 16th c. and the low Gothic tower was replaced by the present high W tower. This has a carillon (by Hemony, 1658) which is among the finest in the country. It is possible to climb to the top of the tower which affords a fine view over Amsterdam.

The interior of the church, now Protestant, has features dating from before the Reformation, including three magnificent windows (1555) from the Dutch High Renaissance, and finely carved wooden choir-stalls.

Location
Ouderkerksplein 23

Trams
4, 9, 16, 24, 25

Times of opening
Mon.–Sat. 11 a.m.–4 p.m.,
Sun. noon–5 p.m.
Closed Jan./Feb.

Many famous citizens of Amsterdam are buried here, including
Rembrandt's wife Saskia and deserving admirals.

Oudemanhuispoort   B3

This arcade has a number of antiquarian bookshops and book-
stalls with "oude mannetjes" (little old men) behind the counter. As its name "old men's gateway" indicates, the arcade
used to be the entrance to an old people's home. Above the
entrance there are still allusions to old age: a pair of spectacles
and two old men. Times of opening Mon.–Sat. 10 a.m.–4 p.m.

Location
Between Grimburgwal and
Kloveniersburgwal

Trams
4, 9, 16, 24, 25

Oudewater

Oudewater, in the Province of Utrecht, is chiefly known for its
"witch scales" (Heksenwaag) from 1595, on which alleged
witches were weighed until 1754 and usually found to be too
heavy. Even in those days very few Dutchwomen would have
weighed less than 50 kg (8 st) on the scales, and if one weighed
more she could not be a witch because otherwise her broom-
stick would have collapsed under her weight. This "witches'
friend" can still be seen today (Leeuweringerstraat 2).
The historical little town with its narrow canals makes a living
today from agriculture, industry and services, although
roughly 60% of the working population have jobs elsewhere.
Oudewater was inhabited as early as the end of the 10th c. and
belonged to the bishopric of Utrecht. It received its charter in
1265 but was pledged to Floris V of Holland in 1280. This pledge
was in fact never redeemed, so that Oudewater remained part
of the Province of South Holland until 1970. The town served
Floris V as a frontier fortress which involved it in many dis-
putes, insurrections and sieges, even in later years.
There was peace, however, in the religious field, so that Oudewater became a haven for many Catholic refugees. Trade and
industry flourished here in the late Middle Ages.
Besides its many old houses with stepped gables, visitors
should also see the 14th c. church (Norderheerkstraat 20),
whose tower has a saddleback roof and carillon (c. 1300), the
town hall (Stadhuis, Visbrug 1) with its Renaissance façade
(restored in 1973).

Location
42 km (26 miles) S

VVV
17 IJsselveere
Tel.0 34 86/14 53
Open in the season:
Mon – Fri. 9.a.m.– 6 p.m.,
Sat.10 a.m.– noon

Times of opening
Mid-April–mid-Sept.: Tues.–
Sat. 10 a.m.–5 p.m., Sun. and
public holidays noon–5 p.m.

Portugese Synagoge (Portuguese synagogue)   D3/4

The Portuguese synagogue, the largest of the three houses of
worship on the J. D. Meijerplein, is reached through a forecourt
surrounded by small houses (including the sexton's house, the
Tes Haim library and the Livraria Montezinos).The building,
completed in 1675 and facing SE towards Jerusalem, was modelled on the temple of Solomon. The finest building of the
Jewish faith in the Netherlands, it contains an ark of the cove-
nant made of rare Brazilian wood and splendid menorahs. The
synagogue was restored between 1953 and 1959.

Location
J. D. Meijerplein

Tram
9

Metro
Waterlooplein

◀ *Oude Kerk: Amsterdam's oldest church*

Prinsengracht

Prinsengracht: gracious living behind old façades

Rembrandthuis

Rembrandt: modelled in wax

Rijksmuseum

Rembrandt's "Night Watch"

Prinsengracht   G5–6/H5–7

The Prinsengracht is less elegant than either the Keizersgracht or the Herengracht (see entries) and therefore livelier and busier. The rents of the houses here are much more reasonable; there are relatively fewer banks and offices but many snug little cafés.

Location
Between Prinsenstraat and Amstelveld

*Rembrandthuis (Rembrandt's house)   C3

Rembrandt, with his wife Saskia, spent his happiest and most successful years when pupils and commissions poured in, in this house on the Jodenbreestraat which is now the Rembrandt museum. It was in this quarter, where Jews had settled (see Jodenbuurt) from all over the world, that he found the models for his Biblical themes. Here he painted what he had seen during the day on his outings along the canals and the Amstel. The house in which Rembrandt lived for about 20 years has again been furnished in the style of the 17th c. and contains numerous etchings and drawings as well as the painter's own personal objects. Admission fee.

Location
Jodenbreestraat 4–6

Tram
9

Metro

Times of opening
Mon.–Sat. 10 a.m.–5 p.m.,
Sun. and public holidays
1–5 p.m.

Rembrandtsplein (Rembrandt Square)   B4 (H6)

Besides the Leidseplein (see entry) the Rembrandtsplein is the most important leisure centre in the city, albeit different in

Location
Centre, near the Amstel

Rijksmuseum

Trams
4, 9

character. There are cafés and eating places here, too, but the Rembrandtsplein is predominantly the quarter for night clubs and striptease establishments.

The square, in which the buttermarket used to be held, has always been a centre of social life. When fairs were held here it swarmed with people in search of the abundance of entertainments to be found in the booths and at the many stalls.

When the buttermarket was discontinued in the mid-19th c. the square retained its atmosphere as somewhere to stroll and find amusement. It was then that it acquired its present name when the little park was laid out with its statue of Rembrandt.

Rijksmuseum (National Museum)   G/H7

Entrances
Stadhouderskade 42

Trams
1, 2, 5

Times of opening
Tues.–Sat. 10 a.m.–5 p.m.;
Sun. and public holidays
1–5 p.m.

Closed
1 Jan. and Mon.

Admission fee

Guided tours
English and French

The world-famous museum of art goes back to the time of King Louis Napoleon who wanted to make Amsterdam a centre for art and science. In 1809 he set up the Grand Musée Royal in his palace (see Koninklijk Paleis) on the Dam (see entry). Works from the national museum in The Hague, which had been opened in 1798, and a few pieces belonging to the city (including Rembrandt's "Night Watch") formed the basis for this museum, which grew swiftly with the purchase of various collections.

Soon the palace rooms could no longer hold all the works, so eight years after its foundation the National Museum was transferred to the Trippenhuis (see entry). More purchases and gifts over the next few years made another move inevitable. It was finally decided that a museum in neo-Gothic should be built on the Stadhouderskade (1877–85). The architect was P. H. J. Cuypers.

Today the Rijksmuseum has about 7 million works of art, including 5000 paintings in over 250 rooms, a library with some 35,000 volumes and about 21,000 auction catalogues. Apart from its unique collection of old masters, it offers an exhaustive account of the development of art and culture in the Netherlands and is especially rich in old Dutch handicrafts, medieval Dutch sculpture and modern Dutch paintings. The Rijksmuseum is divided into several departments, of which only the collection of paintings on the first floor is open all day. The other departments can be visited alternately in the morning or the afternoon from approximately 1 p.m. Details can be obtained by telephone.

Painting

The painting department houses an outstanding collection of Dutch 15th to 19th c. masters (especially those of the 17th c., the heyday of Dutch painting). Frans Hals, Johannes Vermeer, Jan Steen, Pieter de Hooch, Peter Paul Rubens and, of course, Rembrandt are represented here by their greatest works. Non-Dutch painters are grouped according to country; this collection includes such masters as Fra Angelico, Goya and Murillo. Only the most important of the great number of masterpieces can be mentioned here. The most outstanding picture is Rembrandt's "Night Watch", restored after it was slashed in 1975, which is one of the master's largest and most famous compositions (1642); also by Rembrandt are the "Anatomy Lesson of Dr Deijman", the "Staalmeesters", the "Jewish Bride" and the portrait (1634) of the wife of the Rotterdam brewer, Haesje Cleyburg.

Frans Hals is represented by several lively portraits, including the "Merry Drinker" and the picture of the Civic Guard completed by Pieter Codde.

Jan Steen is shown not only as a humorist, with several accomplished paintings, but as a religious painter with his "Christ at Emmaus" and "Adoration of the Shepherds".

Gerhard ter Borch and Gabriel Metsu are also represented, as is Pieter de Hooch with his most outstanding works.

Among the museum's most precious treasures are the works of Jan Vermeer van Delft, including his "Straatje".

The "Mill at Wijk bij Duurstede" by Jacob Ruisdael is the most outstanding landscape.

The 17th c. Flemish painters are represented by Rubens (sketch for the "Crucifixion") and several portraits by Anthony van Dyck.

Among the Italian painters are Crivelli, Bellini and Mantegna, Veronese, Tintoretto and Bassano; and the Spanish painters include Velázquez ("Still Life"), Murillo ("Annunciation", "Madonna and Child"), Cano and Cerezo.

The SW annex contains the collection of later Dutch paintings which, in conjunction with the Stedelijk Museum (see entry), covers the whole range of Dutch 19th c. painting.

The print room specialises in Dutch 16th and 17th c. and French 18th c. drawings and prints. In the library the visitor can be shown all the prints from the national collection, such as Rembrandt's etchings.

Print room

This department displays paintings, model ships, flags, costumes, documents, curios and other items illustrating the political and military history of the Netherlands (altogether about 3000 exhibits). The exhibition is not a chronological account but highlights interrelated topics (which are in chronological order) of fundamental importance in the country's history.
The period covered ranges from the late Middle Ages to the present.

Dutch history

The wide-ranging exhibition of liturgical robes, furniture, tapestries, jewellery, pottery, costumes, dolls' houses, Delft pottery, lace, snuff boxes, etc. presents a picture of life in various periods from the Middle Ages to the early 20th c.

Sculpture and handicrafts

The visitor can see Chinese porcelain and objets d'art from India, South-East Asia and the Far East. Japanese prints are to be found in the print room.

Oriental art

Schiphol Airport (Luchthaven Schiphol)

Schiphol airport is 10 km (6 miles) SW of Amsterdam in the middle of the reclaimed Haarlemmermeer polder, about 4 m (13 ft) below sea level. Charts of 1610 term this area "Shipp Holl" which implies that many ships must have foundered here when it was the Haarlemmermeer.

Schiphol was first used by military aeroplanes for take-off and landing in 1917. In 1920 KLM started flights to London and thus brought Schiphol into the international air traffic network. On 10 May 1940 Schiphol was destroyed by bombing but soon after the war it was rebuilt and extended.

Nowadays over 85 airlines fly from Schiphol to more than 185 destinations in 90 countries. The airport complex includes five

Location
10 km (6 miles) SW (E10)

Rail
From Centraal Station every 15 min.

Schiphol: a "signpost" shows the distances to all the flight destinations

runways, arrival and departure buildings, radar installations and workshops. It ranks fifth among the European airports in terms of passengers (14.5 million a year). Work is underway on a new 90 m/295 ft tower which will form part of the planned extension of the airport to take 20 million passengers by the year 2000.

There are magnificent viewing facilities with good views of all the runways on the roof of the 370 m (405 yd) long and 18 m (20 yd) wide central concourse where passengers board their planes. Part of this walk-way is covered. There are also good views from the comfort of the "Aviorama" restaurant.

Visitors to Schiphol should also take a look at the "Aviodrome" aviation museum (see Practical Information, Museums).

Seasoned air-travellers often make a detour via Schiphol to take advantage of one of the best and cheapest duty-free shops in Europe (40,000 different articles).

Schreierstoren (Wailing tower)   C2

Location
On the corner of Prins
Hendrikkade and
Geldersekade

Buses
18, 21, 22, 28, 32, 33, 34, 35,
39, 47, 49, 56, 67

Trams
1, 2, 4, 5, 9, 13, 16, 17, 24, 25

On the corner of Prins Hendrikkade and Geldersekade, near the main station (see Centraal Station), stands the Wailing Tower, a fragment of the medieval city wall. It was the office of the harbour-master until 1960 when he moved into the Port Administration building. The tower has stood empty since that time. There is some controversy about the real meaning of the name: a gable stone bearing the date 1569 shows a woman crying which gave rise to the idea that this was where the sailors' wives took leave of their husbands when they were about to go back to sea. A second version suggests that the name stems

The Stedelijk Museum's new premises

from the fact that the tower stands astride (schrijlings) a wall called the Kamperhoofd. In 1927 a bronze plaque was placed on the tower to commemorate Henry Hudson who set off from here on 4 April 1609 in his ship "De halve Maan" (Half Moon) on a journey which was to end in the founding of New Amsterdam (New York).

Metro
Centraal Station

Singel

H5/6 (A2–4/B1–2, 4)

The Singel was originally a moat, and the city wall ran where the odd-numbered houses now stand. On the other side of the wall lay Amsterdam's vegetable gardens and meadows (the Torensluis is one of the former passages to the gardens). When the city was enlarged and the wall lost its defensive function, it was demolished (c. 1600) and houses were built on the site.
A walk along this canal is interesting because of the quaint details that emerge: No. 7 is no wider than a front door and is thus the narrowest house in Amsterdam. The bridge at the corner of the Oude Leliestraat has a cell just above water-level where men and women must have been put (separately) to sober up. Of particular architectural interest are Nos. 140–142, designed by the famous architect Hendrik de Keyser. Banning Cocq, the principal figure in Rembrandt's "Night Watch", lived here for a while.

Location
Between Herengracht and Voorburgswal

Trams
1, 2, 4, 5, 9, 16, 24, 25

Finally, not far from the University Library, the "Temple of Wisdom", there is Amsterdam's flower market, the Bloemenmarkt. Partly on houseboats it is like a colourful garden where

Bloemenmarkt
(Mon.–Sat. 9a.m.–5 p.m.)

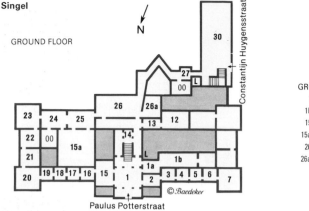

Singel

GROUND FLOOR

Constantijn Huygensstraat

Paulus Potterstraat

© Baedeker

GROUND FLOOR
1 Entrance hall
1b Cloakroom
15 Information
15a Lecture Theatre
26 Restaurant
26a Library/Reading room

The **Stedelijk Museum** (Municipal Museum), founded in 1885, which developed from the *Sophia Augusta De Bruin* foundation, is a *modern art museum* (painting, sculpture, collages, environments, etc.). Only part of the extensive collection is on show at any one time.

Sophia Augusta De Bruin collection: Regency, Louis XV, Louis XVI and Empire interiors; 18th c. kitchen with Delft tiles. Barbizon school: Camille Corot, Charles Daubigny, Gustave Courbet, Honoré Daumier, Aimé Millet, Henri Fantin-Latour, Johann Barthold Jongkind, George Hendrik Breitner, Henri de Toulouse-Lautrec, Edgar Degas, Edouard Manet, Odilon Redon, Paul Gauguin, Paul Cézanne, Claude Monet, James Ensor, Maurice de Vlaminck, Kees van Dongen, Fernand Léger, Edouard Vuillard, Pierre Bonnard, Pablo Picasso, Georges Rouault, Chaim Soutine, Georges Braque, Gino Severini, Raoul Dufy, Elie Delaunay, Marc Chagall, Vassily Kandinski, Ernst Ludwig Kirchner, Oskar Kokoschka, Lovis Corinth, Max Pechstein, August Macke, Paul Klee. De Stijl: Piet Mondrian, Theo van Doesburg. Cobra: Karel Appel, Corneille, Asger Jorn, Pierre Alechinsky, Max Ernst. Action Painting: Jackson Pollock. Pop Art: Roy Lichtenstein, Robert Rauschenberg, Allen Jones, Victor de Vasarely, George Segal, Edward Kienholz. Mobiles by Alexander Calder

FIRST FLOOR

SECOND FLOOR

FIRST FLOOR
114 Print room
(engravings)
114a Print
department
study room
130 New Wing

SECOND FLOOR
201 Sale of
reproductions

L Lift

Stedelijk Museum: exhibition room

you can get all kinds of cut flowers and houseplants, mansize palms included. Every imaginable gardening need is also catered for, ranging from peat, soil, fertiliser and seeds to rakes, hoes, flowerpots and watering cans.

The flower market hasn't always been on the Singel. In the 17th c. it was held every Monday in the summer in St Luciensteeg, near the present-day Amsterdams Historisch Museum (see entry). It must have had a huge selection to offer even then, since one contemporary complained about how difficult and tiresome it was to list all the plants and shrubs on sale.

Stedelijk Museum (Municipal Museum)   G7

The Municipal Museum (founded in 1885) is one of Europe's most important modern art museums. Its collection mainly covers 19th and 20th c. Dutch and French painting.

The museum owes its existence to the appreciation of art and the generosity of leading citizens of Amsterdam. Its collection is based on the gift of the widow Suasso-De Bruin ("Sophia Augusta foundation"). Chr. P. van Eeghen's collection of contemporary art was added to this as well as other collections not confined to contemporary works. These were later transferred to other museums, since in accordance with its original concept the Municipal Museum specialises in modern art from the mid-19th c. onwards.

The following are some of the movements and artists represented:

De Stijl (Van Doesburg, Mondrian, Rietveld), Cobra (Karel Appel, Corneille, Jorn), Colourfield Painting (Kelly, Louis, New-

Location
Paulus Potterstraat 13

Trams
2, 5, 16

Times of opening
Daily 11 a.m.–5 p.m.

man), Pop Art (Rosenquist, Warhol), Nouveau Réalisme (Armand, Spoerri, Tinguely); painters such as Chagall, Dubuffet, De Kooning, Malevitch and Matisse.

The sculpture garden contains numerous works, including those of Rodin, Moore, Renoir, Laurens and Visser.

The Municipal Museum has its own library and puts on avantgarde films, concerts and exhibitions.

Stopera (Stadhuis/Opera) C3/4 (J6)

Location
Waterlooplein
(Amstel 1–3)

Metro
Waterlooplein

Telephone
25 54 55

Much of the former Waterlooplein (see Jodenbuurt) is today taken up with a modern building which houses both Amsterdam's town hall, the "Stadhuis", and its Opera House, "Het Muziektheater" – hence the name "Stopera". Although the Muziektheater was opened in 1986 the Stadhuis wasn't occupied until 1988.

Wilhelm Holzbauer, an Austrian, was responsible for the original plans for this massive building. The L-shaped town hall wraps around the opera house which bulges out, crescentshaped, towards the river and which, with its unusually wide stage (22 m/72 ft) and correspondingly large arena-type auditorium, is the venue for the Dutch national ballet and opera companies, plus guest performances.

Normaal Amsterdams Peil

In the arcade between the town hall and opera house and against the background of a 25 m/82 ft long sectional view of the Netherlands there is a replica of the "Normaal Amsterdams Peil", the NAP. This shows the average water level of the North Sea. The genuine article is actually below the paving in front of the Royal Palace, the Koninklijk Paleis.

Theater Carré B/C4

Location
Amstel 115–125

Trams
4, 9

Telephone
22 52 25

When Amsterdam lost its fair, Oscar Carré, director of the Carré Circus which was exceedingly popular at the turn of the century, began to look for a permanent site in Amsterdam. He found a suitable spot on the Amstel and obtained a temporary permit to build a wooden marquee. However, he ignored the official requirements and had a stone roof put on his marquee. When the municipality ordered him to demolish it he applied for a permanent permit. Eventually he met with success and the Carré in the form we know it today was opened in 1887.

After Oscar Carré's death in 1911 it was converted into a theatre, but this was not as successful as the circus, and in the end the Carré family had to sell the building. It changed hands several times before being transferred in 1927 to a company whose manager, Alex Wunnink, succeeded in re-establishing its importance in Amsterdam's theatre life.

Today all kinds of artistes appear here, plus ballet, musicals and circuses.

Trippenhuis (Trip house) C3

Location
Kloveniersburgwal 29

The elegant mansion, on the corner of the Amstel and the Nieuwmarkt (see entry), was built by the Trip brothers (immen-

Van Gogh museum

sely rich cannon manufacturers) and today houses the Dutch Academy of Sciences.

When the two "cannon kings" moved to Amsterdam they wanted an imposing house to live in. In 1662 they were able to move into the "Trip house" and the chimneys are shaped like the mortars to which the brothers owed their wealth.

Tradition has it that one of the family's servants was heard to say, "Oh, if only I had a house as wide as your front door I should be happy!" One of the Trip brothers overheard this and had a little house built of the same materials and in the same style opposite the Trip house. This little Trip house is still there today at No. 26.

The Royal Institute for Science, Literature and Fine Arts, today the Dutch Academy of Sciences, moved into the Trip house in 1808.

Metro
Nieuwmarkt

Buses
22, 25

*Tropenmuseum (Tropical Museum)   K6

The Tropical Museum, with its displays of art and everyday objects from tropical and sub-tropical areas, is part of the Royal Tropical Institute. Here you can wander round a bazaar, look inside the houses of the Far East and spot the western Coca Cola bottle in the oriental shop. The Museum also hosts regular concerts of Eastern or Asian music and has a large library.

The original purpose of the Royal Tropical Institute, successor to the "Koloniaal Instituut", was to provide information about the Dutch colonies (Surinam, Indonesia and the Dutch Antilles). Nowadays its prime concern is the problems of the Third World.

Location
Linnaeusstraat 2

Bus
22

Tram
9

Opening times
Mon.–Fri.10a.m.–5p.m.;
Sat., Sun. and public
holidays noon–5 p.m.

Universiteit van Amsterdam

TM Junior

The TM Junior Children's Museum is the junior branch of the Tropical Museum. It was re-opened, after lengthy renovations, in 1986 with "the Hour of the Dragon", an exhibition about China, Hong Kong and the Chinese in the Netherlands.

Universiteit van Amsterdam (University)   A3

Location
Spui

Trams
1, 2, 5

The Amsterdam Municipal University, endowed in 1877 and therefore comparatively young, was the first university in the Netherlands after the war to set up a faculty of social and political sciences. It has the reputation of being progressive, and distinguished itself at the time of the student unrest and the "Provo" period in the mid-sixties by its political activities. One of the main university buildings is the former old people's home on the Oudemanhuispoort (see entry).
The "Vrije Universiteit", opened in 1880, is a Christian-oriented university in which teaching is based on the Reformed faith.

**Van Gogh Museum (officially: Rijksmuseum Vincent van Gogh)   G7

Location
Paulus Potterstraat 7

Trams
2, 5, 16

Times of opening
Tues.–Sat. 10 a.m.–5 p.m.;
Sun. and public holidays
1–5 p.m.

Closed
1 Jan. and Mon.

The biggest Van Gogh collection in the world (a donation from Van Gogh's brother Theo and his nephew V. W. Van Gogh), formerly in the Stedelijk Museum (see entry), has been housed since 1972 in the museum specially built for it by Gerrit Rietveld. The collection consists of around 200 paintings, 500 drawings and 700 letters. There are also works by those of Van Gogh's contemporaries who influenced him or were influenced by him. The ground floor of the museum has works from between 1880 and 1887, a period characterised by realistic painting in very dark tones ("The Potato Eaters", 1885).
The first floor shows work from 1887 to 1890 and the pictures glowing with broad brushstrokes of contrasting colour clearly reveal the influence on Van Gogh of the Impressionists. Most were painted in and around Arles ("Vase with Sunflowers", "The Yellow House", "The Sower", etc.).
The second floor has etchings and drawings.
Van Gogh's works on the third floor are arranged thematically along with those of his contemporaries (including Henri Fantin Latour, Henri de Toulouse-Lautrec, Paul Gauguin).
The Museum Library contains literature about Van Gogh and his time. There is also a workshop attached to the museum for teaching aimed at encouraging people to create their own art (e.g. courses in photography, painting and various print techniques).

*Volendam

Location
20 km (12 miles) NE (E10)

Buses
Stop opposite Centraal
Station

The village of Volendam in North Holland is part of the district of Edam (see entry) and lies on the IJsselmeer. As elsewhere, its fishing industry has been hard hit by the damming of the Zuiderzee (see entry).
Volendam is the Catholic counterpart of Marken (see entry). It is famous in the Netherlands for its folk costumes so that it is not surprising that tourism has become its main source of income. The older inhabitants still wear their costumes with pride: for

Volendam: fishermen by the harbour

the men this consists of baggy woollen breeches, while the women wear flowered dresses with striped aprons, coral necklaces, and in cold weather blue-and-white-striped shawls. During the week the women usually wear a simple cheesecloth cap, but on Sundays and holidays this is replaced by the famous lace headdress. From Volendam boat excursions can be made to Marken and Monnickendam.

Besides the harbour and the picturesque old houses the following are of interest:

The wooden church dating from 1685 (restored 1955).

The collection of paintings in the Hotel Spaander by the harbour, with more than 100 works by old masters.

Volendam Museum (Kloostervuurt 5), open daily in summer from 10 a.m. to 5 p.m.

"De Gouden Kamer" (Oude Draaipad 8) which is papered with millions of cigar bands assembled to make pictures such as New York's Statue of Liberty.

In Slobbeland it is possible to see how the houses used to be built on piles.

VVV
21 Zeestraat
Tel. 0 29 93/6 37 47
Open April–Sept. Mon.–Fri.
9 a.m.–5 p.m., Sat./Sun.
10 a.m.–5 p.m.;
Oct.–Mar. Mon.–Fri.
11 a.m.–4 p.m.

De Gouden Kamer
Times of opening
Daily in summer
9 a.m.–6 p.m.

Vondelpark

F/G7

This green lung in the heart of Amsterdam is named after Joost van den Vondel, Holland's most famous poet (see General Information, Famous People). His statue was unveiled in the park in 1867. The park, Amsterdam's Bois de Boulogne as one newspaper called it when it was opened, covers approximately 48 hectares (119 acres) and is landscaped on English lines, with

Location
Main entrance: Leidseplein

Trams
1, 2, 3, 5, 6, 12

Waaggebouw

Waaggebouw on the Nieuwmarkt

sandpits and playgrounds, ponds and fountains, flower-beds and lawns, a rose-garden and a little tea-house, a number of different trees and hedges providing homes for many birds.

At the time of the "Provos" in the mid-sixties the Vondelpark was inhabited by hippies, but when drug-pushing and such attendant crimes as theft became rife, the authorities decided to forbid sleeping in the park at night (see Practical Information, Drugs).

During the summer the park is the venue for the Vondelpark Festival and many other programmes of music, drama and children's events.

Waaggebouw (Weigh-house)   C2

Location
Nieuwmarkt 4

Metro
Nieuwmarkt

The old weigh-house with its seven towers in the Nieuwmarkt (see entry) is the former St Anthony's Gate (St Antoniepoort), once part of the 15th c. city wall. With the growth of the city it was converted in 1617 into the weigh-house and was used to weigh ships' anchors and ordnance as well as foodstuffs.

The upper floor served as the guildhall. Each guild (painters, smiths, surgeons, etc.) had its own entrance. The guild of stonemasons was responsible for its internal and external decoration; the chamber of the guild of bricklayers has been kept in its original state.

In the 17th c. the surgeons gave their lectures on anatomy here and their entrance can still be recognised today by the inscription "Theatrum Anatomicum" above the doorway. Rembrandt was a frequent guest at these lectures which inspired him to paint his "Anatomy Lesson of Dr Tulp" (Mauritshuis,

The Hague) and "Anatomy Lesson of Dr Deijman" (Rijksmuseum).

It was this use that ultimately saved the weigh-house from demolition, since the surgeons needed the building for their work. After 1819 the weigh-house was used for several purposes, including use as a fire-station, for municipal archives and as a museum (see Amsterdams Historisch Museum), it also served as the Jewish Historical Museum until its move in 1987 (see entry). Nowadays it functions as an information and communications centre.

Walletjes

B/C2/3 (H6)

In the oldest part of Amsterdam, between the O.Z. Voorburgwal and the Achterburgwal (see entry), in the triangle formed by the central station, the Dam and the Nieuwmarkt, lie "de Walletjes", the red light district. The "oldest profession" was officially sanctioned here as far back as the 14th c. Along the romantic canals and in the small side alleys the prostitutes sit in their "shop-windows" and offer themselves for sale. If the red light is out and the curtains are drawn the ladies are busy

"De Walletjes" seem strangely sedate with their bizarre mixture of scantily clad girls, sex-shops and little old lady shopkeepers, tourists and locals (not all of whom are clients by any means).

*Westerkerk (West Church)

G5/6

The Westerkerk, in which the magnificent wedding of Princess (now Queen) Beatrix to Claus von Amsberg took place in 1966, is the most popular church in the city. Its tower, popularly known as "Langer Jan" (tall John), which at 85 m (279 ft) is the highest in the city, serves as a symbol of Amsterdam.

After the town went over to Protestantism Hendrick de Keyser began the building in 1620 of the Renaissance church which, uncharacteristically, has many internal and external Gothic features.

After de Keyser's death the building was completed in 1630 by Jacob van Campen and the tower added. On the tip of the spire is the emperor's crown, in memory of Emperor Maximilian of Austria who, in 1489, was cured of an illness in Amsterdam and gave the city his protection and the right to include his crown in its coat of arms. A carillon inside the tower proclaims the hours. Its hammer weighs 200 kg (440 lb) and the largest of the 48 bells weighs 7500 kg (3¼ tons).

The church was consecrated in 1631 with a Whitsun service. The people of the surrounding Jordaan district (see entry) stayed away at first because of the upper classes from along the canals who came here to worship. They wanted a church of their own which they finally acquired with the Noorderkerk.

Besides a fine organ (1622) the church contains an interesting marble column placed there in 1906 in memory of Rembrandt. Rembrandt, who died in poverty, was initially buried outside the church. He was only subsequently reinterred inside the church and his (probably empty) grave is in its northern section (see also Rembrandthuis).

Location
Westermarkt

Buses
21, 67

Trams
13, 17

Times of opening
Church: 1 Apr.–15 Sept.,
Mon.–Sat. 10 a.m.–4 p.m.
Tower: 1 June–15 Sept.,
Tues, Wed., Fri., Sat.
2–5 p.m

Westerkerk: its tower serves as a symbol of Amsterdam

*Zaanse Schans

Location
Zaanstad, 15 km (9 miles) NW (A8)

Rail
From Centraal Station

Times of opening
Apr.–Oct.: daily 9 a.m.–5 p.m.;
Nov.–March: Sat., Sun.
9 a.m.–5 p.m.

About 15 km (9 miles) out of Amsterdam one comes across a little piece of "picture-book Holland": the reconstruction of a Zaanland village as it would have looked about the year 1700. This open-air museum was privately set up in 1948. The Zaanse Schans Foundation managed to rescue old buildings that stood in the way of industrial expansion and typical 17th and 18th c. wooden houses and windmills were dismantled to be re-erected here.

That this open-air museum gives the visitor such a true-to-life picture of the past is due in no small measure to the fact that almost all of the carefully restored houses are inhabited.

At the beginning of the 18th c. this area had about 500 Dutch windmills. Half of them ground mustard, oil, cocoa, spices and tobacco as well as flour. The other half were saw-mills, since the timber industry had been very important in this area in the 17th c. Among the few mills still maintained in Zaanse Schans a dye-mill, a mustard-mill and a sawmill can be visited; there are also a cheese-dairy, an old bakery, an old grocery, a clog-maker's and a pewterer's, as well as the Zaans Museum of Clock-making (Zaanse Uurwerken Museum) with a collection of old Dutch clocks. The old houses and windmills form a delightful backdrop to a boat trip on the Zaans.

Zaanstad

The various places around the River Zaan combine to form the district of Zaanstad.

Location
10 km (6 miles) north (A8)

For four months in 1697 Peter the Great, Tsar of Russia, worked here incognito as a carpenter and shipwright under the name of Peter Michael (an event commemorated by Lortzing in his opera "Zar und Zimmermann"). Those times are recalled by the Tsar Peter House (24 Krimp) and the Tsar Peter Monument on the Dam presented to the town by Tsar Nicholas II in 1911. Also worth a visit are the Old Catholic Church, 1695 (12 Papenpad), the old "Held Josua" sawmill (behind the station), and "de Ooievaar", a watermill dating from 1640 on the southern side of the Julia bridge.
The Zaanse Schans open-air museum (see entry) is just outside Zaandam.

Zaandam

The Zaanlandse Oudheidkamer (80 Lagedijk, open Tues.–Fri. 10 a.m.–noon and 2–4 p.m., Sun. 2–4 p.m.) contains costumes, toys, model ships and other 17th and 18th c. objects and is well worth a visit. There is also the Weefhuis (weaving house) or "house with the picture garden" (39 Lagedijk), the "Death" corn mill (29 Lagedijk), built in 1656, and the Town Hall (104 Lagedijk), an old merchant's house, with antique furniture, frescoes and a collection of stoves.

Zaandijk

The Molen Museum (19 Museumslaan, open Tues.–Fri. 10 a.m.–noon and 2–5 p.m., Sat., Sun. 2–5 p.m.) provides visitors with an account of 17th and 18th c. mills using scale models and documents. A visit to "Het Pink", the old oil mill of 1610 on the Pinkstraat, completes the picture.

Koog aan de Zaan

Places of interest: the Great Church (Torenstraat) with temporary exhibitions in July and August; "het Prinsenhof" (Weelsloot), a mill dating back to 1722; "de Schoolmeester" (Guisweg, 1695), the world's only papermill still in operation; the Stadhuis (Kerkbuurt), a former court-house in the style of Louis XIV, with a cupola (1781); and the "Zuidervermaning" church (231 Zuideinde), with an exceptionally fine interior.

Westzaan

Krommenie has a watermill dating from 1640 and known as "de Woudaap".

Krommenie

There is mention of this, the oldest village on Schermer island, as early as 1325. Its town hall (1613) is worth seeing.

Graft

De Rijp is the birthplace of J. A. Leeghwater, inventor of the diving bell (1575–1650).
Places of interest: the "Wooden House" museum (2 Jan Boonplein; open from Easter to May and Sept./Oct. Sat., Sun. 11 a.m.–5 p.m., from June to August Fri.–Wed. 10a.m.–5p.m.), with displays of tiles, ceramics, old sea-charts and the skeleton of a whale; and the Waagegebouw (2 Kleine Dam), dating from 1690 and the work of Jan van der Heiden, with 24 stained-glass windows.

De Rijp

Purmerend has been an important market town since 1484. The main draw for tourists is the cheese-market every Tuesday

Purmerend

Zandvoort

Zandvoort: seaside resort on Amsterdam's doorstep

from July to September, but the Koepelkerk, with its famous Garrels organ, is also worth seeing.

Broek in Waterland

Broek in Waterland is one of the Netherlands' prettiest villages, its 18th c. wooden houses grouped around a big pond. It still has two cheese-makers and one clogmaker.

Zandvoort

Location
25 km (16 miles) W (A5,A9)

VVV
1 Schoolplein
Tel. 0 25 07/1 79 47
Open in the season:
Mon.–Fri. 9 a.m.–5 p.m.,
Sat.10 a.m.–noon)

Zandvoort is in North Holland on the North Sea and has an international reputation as one of the main Dutch seaside resorts. It gets more than 1½ million overnight visitors a year and is also famous for its motor racing circuit (4.2 km/2.6 miles) which is the setting for the Formula 2 Zandvoort Grand Prix at the end of July and the Formula 1 Holland Grand Prix at the end of August.

Although it has all the attractions of a modern seaside resort Zandvoort tries to preserve its past, and the renovation of the northern part of the town has sought to retain the atmosphere of the old fishing village which, in 1828, had only 700 inhabitants. The Folklore Association and the Old Zandvoort Society also endeavour to keep up the old customs and traditional dress.

Beside its seaside and broad beaches Zaandvoort's attractions include:

its observation tower, 60 m/197 ft high, with a restaurant;

the dolphinarium (2 Burgermeester van Fenemaplein) with dolphins and sealions;

Zandvoort Casino (7 Badhuisplaats), which is on the 18th floor of the "Bouwes", the highest point on the Dutch coast. It's open from 2 p.m. to 2 a.m., and you can try your luck for as little as 5 guilders.

The dunes known as "the Amsterdam Waterworks", which cover 3600 ha./14 sq. miles, are fine for walking, and other sports range from golf and miniature golf to horseriding and tennis.

Zoo

See Artis

Zuiderkerk (south church)   C3

The Zuiderkerk, built between 1603 and 1611 (tower completed 1614) was the first Protestant church to be built in Amsterdam after the Reformation. Its architect was Hendrik de Keyzer, who is also buried here, according to a memorial with verses by Joost van den Vondel (see Famous People). The rectangular basilica-type triple nave church, with six sets of coffer-vaulting, originally had 16 stained-glass windows, but these were removed as early as 1658 to let more light in. The Zuiderkerk ceased to be a church in 1929 and its art treasures were then stored elsewhere. Its most tragic use was in 1944/45 when it served as a temporary mortuary for the many victims of the "Hunger Winter" (memorial tablet on the churchyard wall).

Since 1950 the Zuiderkerk has been used for various exhibitions, particularly by the town planners. After thorough restoration in the late Seventies it is now the centre for local social and cultural activities.

The tower of the Zuiderkerk, which is almost 80 m/262 ft high, is among the finest in Amsterdam. The lower section, which shows a clear list to the south-west of more than a meter, is brick, then comes a section in sandstone, topped finally by a wooden pinnacle covered with lead. The carillon in the octagonal spire is the work of the Hemony brothers. It has been renovated several times and consists of 47 bells, the largest weighing 3300 kg/7277 lbs, ranging over four octaves.

There used to be a cemetery around the Zuiderkerk. One of the two elaborately decorated gateways that provided the entrances to the churchyard has been rebuilt and gives onto the Sint Antoniesbreestraat.

Location
Zandstraat

Metro
Nieuwmarkt

Tower
From June to mid Oct.:
Wed. 2–5 p.m.;
Thurs., Fri. 11 a.m.–2 p.m.;
Sat. 11 a.m.–4 p.m.

*Zuiderzee

Originally the Zuiderzee was a bay in the North Sea. After it was cut off by the Afsluitdijk in 1932 its name was changed to the IJsselmeer. The plan was to reclaim some of the land for industry and agriculture and for use as residential areas. Some of the polders, as the reclaimed areas are called, are already in use: the Wieringermeer polder, covering 20,000 hectares (49,420 acres) was reclaimed as early as 1930; the Noordoostpolder (1942) covers 48,000 hectares (118,608 acres), and the reclamation of the East Flevoland polder (54,000 hectares – 133,434 acres) and the South Flevoland polder (43,000 hectares –

106,253 acres) was completed in 1957 and 1968 respectively. Lelystad in East Flevoland is to become a residential and industrial centre of national importance.

There are plans to build the towns of Almere and Zeewolde in South Flevoland. The primary objective of these polders and of the Markerwaard which has yet to be reclaimed is to reduce the pressure of population on the surrounding conurbations. They will be residential, employment and recreational areas. The remaining lakes around the edges are becoming the sites of swimming pools, camp-sites and marinas. Last but not least, the polders enable important lines of communication to be set up – for example, between the provinces of North Holland and Friesland.

Visitors who are interested in the land-reclamation project should visit the Enkhuizen Zuidersee Museum (see Practical Information, Museums concerning land-reclamation).

A permanent exhibition about the land reclamation process is housed in a display building near the harbour.

Practical Information A to Z

**NOTE: From March 1991 all Amsterdam six figure telephone
numbers are due to be prefixed by an extra 6.**

Accommodation

See Camping, Hotels and Motels, Youth Hostels

Advance Booking

Stadsschouwburg
Corner of Marnixstraat/Leidseplein. Advance ticket sales for all
Amsterdam's concerts, plays, ballet, etc. Free monthly events
programme. Open: Mon.–Sat. 10 a.m.–6 p.m.

Theater Bespreek Bureau, Stationsplein 10
Open: Mon.–Sat 10 a.m.–4 p.m.

Airlines

Air France
Strawinskylaan 813, tel. 5 73 15 11

Air UK
Postbus/PO Box 12010
3004 GA Rotterdam, tel. (010) 37 02 11

Australian Airways/Quantas
Stadhouderskade 6, tel. 83 80 81

Canadian Pacific
Leidsestraat 55, tel. 22 44 44

KLM
Leidseplein 1, tel. 47 47 74 7

Pan Am
Leidseplein 31c, tel. 26 20 21

SAA/SAL
Stadhouderskade 2, tel. 16 44 44

Airport (Luchthaven)

Schiphol, Amsterdam's airport (see entry, Amsterdam A to Z),
is about 16 km/10 miles SW of the city near the E10 motorway
from Amsterdam to The Hague.
A direct rail link connects it to the Central Station (Centraal
Station).

Antiques (Antieken)

There are a great many antique shops centred around the
Nieuwe Spiegstraat, Spiegelgracht, Rokin and Elandsgracht.

Centres

Auction Houses

Prices for top items are no cheaper here than in the other big European cities.

Selection of shops

Amsterdam Antiques Gallery
Nieuwe Siegelstraat 34

A. van de Meer
P. C. Hooftstraat 112
Fine prints

Premsela en Hamburger
Rokin 120
Jewellry, gold and silver

E. Wassenaar
Hobbemnastraat 10a
Jewellry

1900–1930
Keizersgracht 347
Art Nouveau

Ingrid Vos
Lijnbaansgracht 290
Art Nouveau

Markets

Antiekmarkt De Looier
Elandsgracht 109
Open: Mon.–Thurs., Sat. 11 a.m.–5 p.m.

From April to mid-October there is an art market on the Thorbeckeplein on Sundays from noon to 6 p.m.

Flea market

See Amsterdam A to Z, Jodenbuurt

Auction Houses (Veilingen)

The following auction houses handle antiques, furniture, objets d'art and books:
Christies, Cornelis Schuytstraat 57
De Eland, Elandsgracht 68
A. W. Mastenbroek, Leidsegracht 76
Mak van Waay, Rokin 102
De Zwaan, Keizersgracht 474

Banks

Opening times

Mon.–Fri. 9 a.m.–4 p.m.
Some banks are open till 9 on late-night shopping Thursdays.
The Algemene Bank Nederland at Schiphol airport is open daily from 7 a.m. to midnight.

Outside normal business hours money can be changed at the following exchange offices:

GWKs
(Grenswisselkantoren)

Central Station: Mon.–Sat. 7 a.m.–10.45 p.m., Sun. 8 a.m.–10.45 p.m.

Amstel Station: Mon.–Sat. 8 a.m.–8 p.m., Sun. 10 a.m.–4 p.m.
KLM House, Leidseplein: Mon.–Fri. 8.30 a.m.–5.30 p.m., Sat.
10 a.m.–2 p.m.
Schiphol airport: Mon.–Sat. 8 a.m.–8 p.m., Sun. 10 a.m.–4 p.m.

Damrak 17: daily 8 a.m.–midnight
Damrak 86: daily 8 a.m.–11.45 p.m.
Kalverstraat 150: daily 8 a.m.– 8 p.m.
Leidsestraat 106: daily 8 a.m.–midnight

Change Express
Exchange Offices

Dam 23-25: daily 8.30 a.m.–10 p.m.
Leidseplein 31a: daily 8.30 a.m.–10 p.m.
Damrak 20: daily 8.30 a.m.–10 p.m.

Thomas Cook
Exchange Offices

Baths

See Swimming

Bicycle Hire (fietsverhuur)

The easiest way to get to know Amsterdam is to do what the
locals do and get on your bike. Bikes can be hired on a daily or
weekly basis, although the rates are not particularly cheap. The
following are some of the firms hiring out those famous Dutch
bikes.

Fiets-O-Fiets, Amstelveenseweg 880–900, tel. 44 54 73
Heja, Bestevaerstraat 39, tel. 12 92 11
Koenders, Utrechtsedwarsstraat 105, tel. 23 46 57
Koenders rent a bike, Stationsplein 33, tel. 24 83 91

Bookshops (boekwinkel)

Nearly all Dutch bookshops sell the original English-language
versions of English and American books.

English Bookshop Club
Leidsestraat 52

Athenaeum
Spui 14
Books and magazines

Erasmus
Spui 2
Art books, books on antiques

Allert de Lange
Pieter C. Hooftstraat 57
Literature and travel guides

De Kookboekhandel
Runstraat 26

Cookbooks

See Amsterdam A to Z, Oudemanhuispoort

Book market

Business Hours

See Opening Times

Cafés

Dutch cafés have much in common with English pubs. Amsterdam is famous for its "brown cafés" (bruine kroegen), which get their name from their dark, tobacco-stained interiors.

A selection:

De Balie
Leidseplein
Open: from 4 p.m.
Rendezvous for artists from the De Balie Theatre, a former prison.

De Engelbewaarder
Kloveniersburgwal 59
Open: 11 a.m.–1 a.m.
Literary café; also talks and live music

Frascati
Nes 59
Open: Mon.–Sat. 10 a.m.–1 a.m. Sun. from 5 p.m.
Artists' café with theatrical events

Karperschoek
Martelaarsgracht 2
Open: Mon.–Fri. 7 a.m.–1 a.m. Sat. and Sun. 8 a.m.–1 a.m.
Oldest café in Amsterdam; very popular

Mulder
Weteringsschans 163
Open: 8.30 a.m.–1 a.m.
Genever (gin) from the barrel

De Prins
Prinsengracht 124
Open: 11 a.m.–1 a.m.
Café furnished like a drawing-room

Reijnders
Leidseplein 6
Open: 9 a.m.–1 a.m.
Artists' rendezvous with old interior

Schelteme
Nieuwe Zijdsvoorburgwal 242
Open: 8 a.m.–11 p.m.
Haunt of journalists

't Schmackzeyl
Brouwersgracht 101
Open: 9 a.m.–11 p.m.
Canal House

Welling
J. W. Brouwerstraat 32
Open: noon–1 a.m.
Living-room atmosphere

Bim Huis   For jazz fans
Oude Schans 73
Open: before and after concerts; frequented by jazz fans and
musicians

't Doktertje
Rozeboomsteg 4
Open: 4 p.m.–1 a.m.

Schachcafé   For chess players
Korte Leidsewartstraat
Open: 9 a.m.–midnight

Hotel Americain   Pleasant atmosphere
Leidseplein
Art Nouveau interior
Open: 9 a.m.–midnight

Bodega Keyzer
Van Baerlestraat 96
opposite the Concertgebouw
Open: 9 a.m.–midnight
Artistes' rendezvous

Calendar of Events

Horecava: international fair for the hotel and catering trade   January

25 February: commemoration of the strike in February 1941 by   February
Dutch workers protesting against the deportation of their
Jewish compatriots

Hiswa international watersport exhibition   March

30 April: Koninginnedag (the Queen's Birthday). The whole city   April
is in a festive mood with music and bring and buy sales, with
everyone, including the children, joining in. 30 April was originally the birthday of Queen Juliana, and her daughter, Queen
Beatrix, has kept the same date although her own birthday is in
fact on 31 January

Also in April:
Ideal Home Exhibition
World Press Photo Exhibition

4 May: Commemoration of those who died in the Second   May
World War, with a two-minute silence at 8 p.m. throughout the
Netherlands

5 May: Day of Liberation (the German Occupation ended on 5
May 1945), with local celebrations in various parts of the city

Saturday before Whitsun:
Luilak (literally "lazybones"), when children ring doorbells and
make a lot of noise to wake up lie-a-beds and lazybones

	Also in May: Pasar Malam (Indonesian market)
June	Festival of Fools (in summer, in even numbered years)
	Holland Festival Vondelpark Openluchttheater (open-air theatre): Children's theatre, music and dancing, etc. Summer Evening Concerts in the Concertgebouw (until August)
July	Ballet Festival of the National Ballet Summer Festival: Performances in Amsterdam's smaller theatres
September	1st Saturday in September: Floral Procession from Aalsmeer to Amsterdam Street Festival in the Jordaan quarter
November	3rd Saturday in November: Entry of Saint Nicholas (Sinterklaas), who arrives by boat in front of the Centraal Station from "Spain", with his followers and, riding on a white horse, leads his procession through the city to the cathedral where he is welcomed by the Lord Mayor
	Also in November: Europoort Harbour Exhibition
December	5 December, Sinterklaas (Saint Nicholas Day celebrations): Public holiday when presents are exchanged as happens on Christmas Day in English-speaking countries
	Kerstflora (Christmas flora)

Camping

	The campsites in and around Amsterdam are among the cheapest forms of accommodation in what is otherwise an expensive city in that respect.
Campsites	Camping Amsterdamse Bos Kleine Noorddijk 1, Aalsmeer, tel. 020/41 68 68 Open: 1 April–31 October
	Camping Vliegenbos Meeuwenlaan 138, tel. 020/36 88 55 (municipal camp site) Open: 1 April–30 September
	Camping Houtrak Halfweg, tel. 023/38 24 24 Open: 1 May–1 September
	Gaasper Camping Loosdrechtdreef 7, Gaasperdam, tel. 020/96 73 26 (separate section for youngsters) Open: all year

Canal bikes (grachtenfiets)

"Canal bikes" are two–four person pedallos in which you can explore Amsterdam's canals on your own. Four possible routes are described in a leaflet you get given when you hire your "bike". It also tells you the "rules of the road" that have to be observed once you're part of the traffic like any other vessel!

Leidseplein (between Marriott Hotel and Hotel Americain)   Landing stages
Stadhouderskade (between Rijksmuseum and Heineken Brouwerij)
Prinsengracht at the Westerkerk (near Anne Frank Huis)
Keizersgracht (corner of Leidsestraat)
You can return your boat to the landing stage of your choice.

Canal trips

See Sightseeing

Car Rental

Nassaukade 380, tel. 83 60 61   Avis
Schiphol airport, tel. 60 41 301

Overtoom 121, tel. 12 60 66   Budget
Schiphol airport, tel. 17 53 88

Overtoom 51–53, tel. 83 21 23   Europcar/InterRent
Schiphol airport, tel. 60 41 566

Overtoom 333, tel. 85 24 41   Hertz
Schiphol airport, tel. 17 08 66

Chemists (apotheken)

Mon.–Sat. 8 a.m.–5.30 p.m.   Opening times

Ring 64 21 11 for information on chemists that are open in the   Emergency service
evening, at night and at weekends.
A list of which chemists are providing an emergency service is available in chemists' shops, and the address of the nearest chemist that is open is displayed on the door of chemists that are closed.

Church Services

Christ Church   Church of England
Groenburgwal 42, tel. 24 00 77
Sun. 9.30 a.m., 10.30 a.m. and 7.30 p.m.

Church of Scotland   Presbytarian
Begijnhof 48, tel. 24 96 65
Daily 10.30 a.m., Wed. 12.40 p.m. and 1.10 p.m., Sun. 9.30 a.m., 10.30 a.m. and 7.30 p.m.

Begijnhofkerk   Roman Catholic
Begijnhof 35, tel. 22 19 18
Service in English: noon

Cinemas (bioscoop)

All foreign films are screened in the original language version, with Dutch sub-titles. Programmes change on Thursdays. Details are given in the press. See also Programme of Events.

Cinemas

Alfa 1, 2, 3, 4
Hirschgebouw, Leidseplein, tel. 27 88 06

Alhambra 1, 2
Weteringschans 134, tel. 23 31 92

Bellevue Cinerama
Marnixstraat 400, tel. 23 48 76

Calypso 1, 2
Marnixstraat 402, tel. 26 62 27

Centraal
Nieuwendijk 67, tel. 24 89 33

Cineac
Regulierbreestraat 31, tel. 24 36 39

Cinecenter
(Coraline, Filmhuis Jean Vigo, Peppe Nappa, Pierrot)
Lijnbaansgracht 236, tel. 23 66 15

Cinema International 2
Aug. Allebéplein 4, tel. 15 12 43

City 1, 2, 3, 4, 5, 6, 7
Kleine Gartmanplantsoen (near Leidseplein), tel. 23 45 79

Kriterion
Roeterstraat 170, tel. 23 17 08

The Movies
Haarlemmerdijk 161, tel. 24 57 90

Parisien
Nieuwendijk 69, tel. 24 89 93

Rembrandsplein Theater 1, 2
Rembrandtsplein, tel. 22 35 42

Studio K
Roeterstraat 34, tel. 23 17 08

Theater Tuschinksi 1, 2, 3, 4, 5, 6
Regulierbreestraat 26, tel. 26 26 33

In art nouveau, this is reckoned to be Europe's finest and best preserved movie palace.

De Uitkijk
Prinsengracht 452, tel. 23 74 60

Concert Halls

See Theatres, Concert Halls

Consulates

Australian Consulate
Koninginnegracht 23
The Hague. Tel. (070) 63 09 83
Open: Mon.–Fri. 9 a.m.–1 p.m., 2–5 p.m.

Australia

Canadian Consulate
Sophialaan 7
The Hague. Tel. (070) 61 41 11

Canada

South African Consulate
Wassenaarseweg 40
The Hague. Tel. (070) 92 45 01

South Africa

British Consulate
Koningslaan 44
Tel. 76 43 43
Open: Mon.–Fri. 9.30 a.m.–12.30 p.m., 2.30–4.30 p.m.

United Kingdom

American Consulate
Museumplein 19
Tel. 79 03 21
Open: Mon.–Fri. 9 a.m.–noon, 2–4 p.m.

United States of America

Currency

The unit of currency is the Dutch guilder (hfl) which consists of 100 cents. There are banknotes for 5, 10, 25, 50, 250 and 1000 hfl, and coins in denominations of 5 (stuiver), 10 (dubbeltje), 25 (kwartje) cents and 1 hfl (guilder), 2.50 (rijksdaalder) and 5 hfl.

Unit of currency

There are no restrictions on the import or export of local or foreign currency.

Currency import/export

Banks, big hotels, restaurants and shops will take Eurocheques, travellers' cheques and most international credit cards.

Cheques, credit cards

See Banks

Changing money

Customs Regulations

Certain items for personal use can be imported duty-free. In addition persons over 15 years of age can take in 1000 g coffee or 400 g instant coffee and 200 g tea or 80 g teabags, and persons over 17 can take in 1.5 litres spirits over 22% or 3 litres spirits under 22% or 3 litres sparkling wine and 5 litres wine, plus 300 cigarettes or 75 cigars or 400 g tobacco. Persons over 15 may also take in goods and presents up to a total value of

On entry

890 hfl.
The importing of weapons is forbidden.

On departure | No restrictions.

Currency import/export | There are no restrictions on the import or export of local or foreign currency.

Re-entry into the United Kingdom | For goods bought in the Netherlands the current European Community allowances will apply.

Department Stores

De Bijenkorf
Damrak 90
Amsterdam's oldest department stores with the broadest range and better quality goods

Vroom & Dreesmann
Kalverstraat (near Munt tower)
Bilderdijkstraat 37–51
Bos en Lommerweg 357–359
Department store chain, not as exclusive as the Bijenkorf

Hema
Nieuwendijk 174, etc.
Cheap department store chain

Maison de Bonneterie
Rokin 140

Metz & Co.
Keizersgracht 455

Specialist shops | See Shopping

Diamonds

Amsterdam already had a lively developing diamond trade in the 16th c. and, with the discovery of diamonds in South Africa in 1867, most of which were cut in Amsterdam, this trade expanded and the city became one of the world's most important diamond centres. The supreme skill of Amsterdam's diamond cutters and polishers (see Amsterdam A–Z, Diamond cutting) had an important part to play in this. To the connoisseur the phrase "Amsterdam Cut" is synonymous with perfect cutting.

Rough Diamonds | Diamonds (from the Greek word "adamas" meaning invincible) are among the most valuable of precious stones. They are pure carbon crystals, mostly octahedron or dodecahedron, and only rarely cubic, in shape, and extremely hard.

Sources | Diamonds occur in basic and ultrabasic rocks (Kimberlite; workings down to 2000 m (6600 ft) below the ground) and in alluvial deposits. The world's main sources of diamonds are in Africa (Zaire, South Africa, Ghana, Sierra Leone, South West

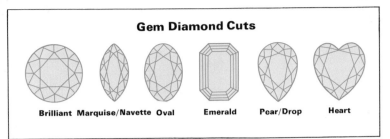

Gem Diamond Cuts

Brilliant Marquise/Navette Oval Emerald Pear/Drop Heart

Africa/Namibia, Botswana, Tanzania, Liberia, Central Africa, Ivory Coast, Angola), the USSR (Urals), South America (Venezuela, Brazil, Guyana) and Indonesia and the East Indies.

More than three quarters of the diamonds found are used for industrial purposes (drills, stone and glass cutters; drilling, grinding, lapping, polishing; precision instruments, etc.) and barely a quarter are taken for jewellery. Since 1955 it has been possible to manufacture synthetic diamonds for industrial purposes. *Uses*

The four factors determining the value of a gem diamond, also known as "the four Cs", are its colour, clarity, cut and carat weight. *Value*

The brilliant cut is the best known and most favoured type of cutting and consequently the cut and polished diamonds are usually called brilliants, but strictly speaking this only applies to diamonds where the full cut is in 58 facets. The Marquise (Navette), Oval, Emerald, Drop and Heart cuts also each have 58 facets. Other cuts are the Baguette (simple cut with 24 facets), Octahedron (16 facets) and Carré (a square cut).
Facets are the surfaces created by cutting, which must be arranged at certain angles to each other in order to obtain the optimum refraction of light. The largest horizontal facet is called the "table" *Cut*

The colours are known by the following terms. *Colour*
River – pure-white (blue-white)
Top Wesselton – clear white
Wesselton – white
Top Crystal – slightly tinted white
Crystal – tinted white
Top Cape – considerably tinted white, pale yellowish
Cape (Light Yellow) – yellowish
Diamonds in clear, strong colours such as yellow, brandy-brown, rose, green or blue are the most highly valued.

The degree of clarity (recognisable under ×10 magnification): *Clarity*
Internally Flawless, no inclusions
V.V.S.I. – very, very small inclusions
S.I. – small inclusions
I Piqué – visible inclusions
II Piqué – larger inclusions
III Piqué – large inclusions

The weight of a diamond is measured in carats (1 ct=0·2 g). The word "carat" came originally from Arabic and referred to the *Carat Weight*

Diamond cutters at work

dried red-currant seed, used in earlier times for weighing diamonds in India and gold in Africa. The word carat came, via its Dutch use, to enter the language of international trade as a jeweller's measure. Carats, abbreviated as "ct", are used to express the weight of precious stones (1 metric carat=200 mg) and also the purity of alloys, i.e. the content of gold in alloys (24 ct=pure gold; 18 ct=750/1000; 14 ct=585/1000 parts of gold).

Famous Diamonds

The largest brilliant is the Cullinan I (530 ct) in the Crown of England; it was part of the largest rough diamond ever found (Cullinan, 3106 ct), which was cut into 105 stones. Other famous large diamonds or brilliants include the Excelsior (rough 955 ct, split up into 22 brilliants, weighing 374 ct altogether); the Jonker (rough 726 ct, split up into 12 brilliants); the Nizzam of Hyderabad (polished 340 ct); the Grand Mogul (polished 280 ct); the Jubilee (rough 651 ct, polished 245 ct); the Star of Yacutia (232 ct); the Orloff (polished 200 ct); the Victoria (rough 469 ct, polished 184 ct); the Koh-i-Nor ("Mountain of Light", rough 191 ct, polished 186 ct); the Regent (rough 410 ct, polished 140 ct); and the Florentine (137 ct).

Diamond Cutting

The following diamond cutters cater for visiting groups and individuals.

Amsterdam Diamond Center B.V.
Rokin 1–5, tel. 24 57 87
Trams: 4, 9, 24, 25

Open: Mon.–Wed., Fri., Sat. 10 a.m.–5.30 p.m.; Thurs. 10 a.m.–8.30 p.m.; Sun. 10.30 a.m.–5.30 p.m.

AS Bonebakker & Zoon B.V.
Rokin 86–90, tel. 23 22 94
Trams: 4, 9, 16, 24, 25
Open: Mon.–Fri. 9.30 a.m.–5.30 p.m.; Sat., Sun. 10.30 a.m.–5 p.m.

Coster Diamonds B.V.
Paulus Potterstraat 2–4, tel. 76 22 22
Trams: 1, 2, 16, 24, 25
Open: Mon.–Sat. 9.a.m.–5 p.m., Sun. 10 a.m.–5 p.m.

Diamonds Bab Hendriksen
Weteringschans 89, tel. 26 27 98
Trams: 16, 24, 25
Open: Mon.–Sat. 9 a.m.–6 p.m.; Sun. 10 a.m.–6 p.m.

Gassan Diamond House
Nieuwe Achtergracht 17–23, tel. 22 53 33
Metro: Weesperplein; buses: 5, 55
Open: Mon.–Sun. 9 a.m.–5 p.m.

Holshuysen-Stoeltie B.V.
Wagenstraat 13–17, tel. 23 76 01
Trams: 4, 9
Open: Mon.–Sun. 9 a.m.–5 p.m.

River Diamonds Center
Weteringschans 79a, tel. 27 52 55
Trams: 16, 24, 25
Open: Mon.–Sun. 9 a.m.–5 p.m.

Van Moppes Diamonds
Albert Cuypstraat 2–6, tel. 76 12 42
Trams: 16, 24, 25
Open: Mon.–Sun. 8.30 a.m.–5 p.m. (closed Sun. in winter)

N.B. Opening times often cut short in the winter season.

Doctors

Anyone requiring help (doctor, dentist, chemist) should dial 64 21 11. The caller will be given details of the doctor, dentist or chemist available. This service operates day and night.

Medical Assistance

Tel. 5 55 55 55.

Ambulance

Visitors from abroad and members of their families can claim medical attention according to Dutch medical insurance regulations, providing three conditions are fulfilled:
1. The visitor must come from a country with which the Netherlands has an international agreement in this field.
2. Medical attention must be urgently needed and promptly claimed in the manner customary in the Netherlands.
3. An international medical form (or a photocopy) must be given to the doctor, hospital or chemist.

Out-patient Treatment

The account is settled directly between the doctor, hospital or chemist and the ANOZ Medical Insurance Bureau. Visitors are

Settlement of Claims

therefore advised to have with them a few copies of the international medical insurance form (in Great Britain E.111), to be able to give a copy to the appropriate authority. It will not normally be necessary to settle the account personally.

Invalid Transport ANOZ

The relevant authority for the international agreement in the Netherlands is the foreign section of the ANOZ Medical Insurance Bureau, Kaap Horndreef 24–28, 3506 GB Utrecht, tel. 030/61 88 81.

Hospitals

See entry

Documents

See Travel documents

Drugs

Drugdealing and drugtaking is forbidden by law. You can be fined for being in possession of less than 30 g of marijuana, and imprisoned for anything in excess of that amount. Nevertheless Amsterdam still has 8000–10,000 heroin addicts to cope with, and drug dealing goes hand in hand with a rising crime rate. The Amsterdam authorities are doing their best to tackle the problem of drugs in their city and in fact the notorious Zeedijk, where dealing had been centred, has been cleaned up thanks to non-stop police patrols. This sort of action is intended to make it clear to foreign "junkies" that they're not wanted in Amsterdam.

Drug counselling

Jongeren Advies Centrum (JAC)
Amstel 30, tel. 24 29 49
Open: Mon., Tues., Thurs., Fri. 10 a.m.–noon; Wed., Sat., Sun. 7–10 p.m.
The JAC also provides youngsters with free and anonymous legal aid, and helps with medical and psychological problems.

Consultatiebureau voor Alcohol en Drugs
Keizersgracht 812, tel. 23 78 65
Open: Mon.–Fri. 1–3 p.m.

The Federatie van Instellingen voor Alcohol en Drugs (Federation of Institutions for Alcohol and Drugs) can provide further information on help from other organisations (tel. 030/78 07 24).

Doctors

See entry

Dutch Cuisine

Anyone who chooses one of Amsterdam's many restaurants (see entry) that offer the local specialities will soon discover that Dutch cooking is filling but not too heavy.

Hotpots

The simple, substantial Dutch hotpot is mostly potatoes and greens, plus tasty chunks of meat and diced bacon. The "Hutspot'' is a popular variation made up of equal proportions of potatoes, onions and carrots. Thick green pea soup (erwtensoep) is a staple national dish in the winter months.

Pancake (pannekoeken) houses offer an infinite variety of sweet and savoury pancakes, with syrup, apple, liqueur, salami, ham, cheese, mushrooms or bacon. On the "poffertje" stalls hot, fresh small pancakes-cum-doughnuts are fried in cast-iron pans and sold dipped in icing sugar with a knob of butter.

Pancakes

One of the typical Dutch delicacies is, of course, the herring which can be bought at the fishmonger's or eaten on the spot, with or without onions, at one of the many herring stalls.

Herring

A speciality of the "broodjeswinkels" – which are shops selling fresh bread rolls with a variety of different fillings – is the "broodje half om" which has salted meat on one half and thinly sliced cooked liver on the other. Another speciality is a roll with "tartar" or raw minced beef, and boiled egg.

"broodje half om"

Liquorice fans will be delighted by the many different kinds of "drop", the Dutch liquorice, and suiting every taste from sweet to salty. Those who like old fashioned sweeties such as sticks of rock, jelly babies and candy will find plenty to choose from in the sweetshops. Another sweet delicacy is the "Amsterdammertje", a cake stuffed with marzipan.

Sweets

Emergencies

Tel. 22 22 22	Police
Tel. 64 21 11	Doctors, dentists
Tel. 21 21 21	Fire brigade
Tel. 5 55 55 55	Hospital emergency

Food and Drink

It is hard to go hungry in Amsterdam. Besides the hearty Dutch cuisine (see entry), the visitor will find an infinite number of speciality restaurants.
If you lack the time or the money to eat in restaurants there is plenty of cheap food to be had; for instance a filled roll from one of the shops called "broodjes" or a snack from the stalls selling fish, etc. on street corners or in the markets (see entry).

The typical Dutch drinks are beer and genever (gin). An "oude genever" (old gin) is stronger than a "jonge genever" (young gin). The tots of gin (borreltjes) are also served with ice or as long drinks with Coca Cola or tonic water. Imported drinks such as whisky or wine are much more expensive than the local spirits.

Drink

In the "tasting bars", where the principal drinks served are brandy and liqueurs, the glasses are filled so full, that it is

Alcohol Tasting Bars

necessary to bend down to take the first sip; if the glass is moved the drinker runs the risk of spilling the precious liquid! Every visitor should try this at least once.
Continental Bodega (Sherry Bodega), Lijnbaansgracht 246
De Drie Fleschjes, Gravenstraat 18 (closed Sun.)
Hooghoudt, Reguliersgracht 11 (closed Sun.)
Wijnand Fockink, Pijlsteeg 31 (closed Sun.)

Food Shops

See Specialist shops

Galleries

Amsterdam has a great many galleries, so those that follow are just a selection, and a stroll along the canals will also reveal any number of small exhibitions.

Amazone, Keizersgracht 678, tel. 27 90 00
Artigalerie, Spui 1a, tel. 23 35 08
Art & Project, Prinsengracht 785, tel. 22 03 72
Asselijn, Lange Leidsedwarsstraat 198–200, tel. 24 90 30
Bais, Van Baerlestraat 100, tel. 71 88 08
Brinkmann, Kerkstraat 105, tel. 22 74 93
Cheiron, P. C. Hooftstraat 153, tel. 64 58 13
Collection d'Art, Keizersgracht 516, tel. 22 15 11
Espace, Keizersgracht 548, tel. 24 08 02
Forum, Herengracht 156, tel. 26 52 07
Hamer, Leliegracht 38, tel. 26 73 94
Hologrammen, Prinsengracht 675, tel. 22 97 49
Jurka, Singel 28, tel. 26 67 33
Krikhaar, Spuistraat 330, tel. 26 71 66
Mokum, Oudezijds Voorburgwal 334, tel. 24 39 58
Printshop, Prinsengracht 845, tel. 25 16 56
Siau, Keizersgracht 267, tel. 26 76 21

Getting to Amsterdam

By Car

A number of companies operate ferries between Great Britain and the Netherlands and it is advisable to find out from your travel agent which crossing is the most suitable for your needs. Crossings include:
Sealink ferry from Harwich to Hoek van Holland
North Sea ferries from Hull to Rotterdam
Car ferry service from Sheerness to Vlissingen
Norfolk Line from Great Yarmouth to Scheveningen
P & O ferries from Felixstowe to Zeebrugge (Belgium)

By Coach

Travel by coach is becoming increasingly popular and Amsterdam is a favourite destination for city tours. Many companies offer a variety of inexpensive tours and there are regular coach services to Amsterdam from London and certain other towns and cities in Britain. Check with your local travel agent.

By Air

There are connections between Amsterdam's main airport, Schiphol, and all major U.S. and European airports. A direct service links the airport to the Centraal Station by rail.

The main rail service is via the Sealink ferry between Harwich and Hoek van Holland. Further details and reservations are available.

In the UK from:
British Rail
Liverpool Street Station
London EC2. Tel. 071–247 7600

Netherlands Railways
4 New Burlington Street
London SW1. Tel. 071–734 3301

In Amsterdam from:
Nederlands spoorwegen
Stationsplein
Tel. 020 25 51 51

British Rail
Leidseplein 5
Tel. 020 23 41 33

The Central Station in Amsterdam has tourist information centres (VVV), exchange bureaux, taxis, tram and bus connections. Information regarding fares, timetables and overnight accommodation can be obtained from British Rail.

Pre-booking of a hotel room, even in student hotels, can be made through:
Nationaal Reserveringscentrum (NRC)
O.O. Box 404
2260 AK Leidschedam
Tel. 070/20 25 00

Hotel Reservations

Handicapped Visitors

A special brochure for handicapped visitors to the Netherlands can be obtained from the Dutch Tourist Offices (see Information)

Hospitals (ziekenhuis)

Academisch Medisch Centrum
Meibergdreef 9, tel. 5 66 91 11

Casualty services

Onze Lieve Vrouwe Gasthuis
1e Oosterparkstraat 179, tel. 5 99 91 11

Sint Lucas Ziekenhuis
Jan Tooropstraat 164, tel. 5 10 89 11

Slotervaartziekenhuis
Louwesweg 6, tel. 5 12 93 33

Stichting Kruispost
O.Z. Voorburgwal 129, tel. 24 90 31

V.U. Ziekenhuis
de Boelelaan 1117, tel. 5 48 91 11

Hotels

	Ziekenhuis Amsterdam-Noord Distelkade 21, tel. 36 89 22
Children's clinic	Emma Kinderziekenhuis Spinozastraat 51, tel. 22 02 80
Dental clinic	Tandheelkunde Instituut Louwesweg 1, tel. 15 60 62
Drug counselling	See Drugs
Emergencies	See entry

Hotels

Reservations

The VVV (Tourist Information Centres, see Information) can help you find a suitable hotel, but you have to call by in person. They also provide a free hotel guide and can help you book accommodation in other places outside Amsterdam. Anyone planning to visit Amsterdam for peak public holidays like Easter or Whitsun should book accommodation in good time, either with the hotel direct or through the National Reserverings Centrum (Postbox 404, 2260 AK Leidschendam, tel. 070/20 25 00.

Categories

Hotels are officially divided up into five categories ranging from five-star (luxury) and three-star (very comfortable) to one-star (modest).
The following list is drawn up according to these categories, and gives the number of beds (B) along with the hotel address and telephone number.

Prices

The following prices, which are in Dutch guilders, are the average for one night and include breakfast, service and tax. Out of season, particularly in the winter, it is possible to get rates that are considerably lower.

Hotel categories

	single room	double room
*****	300–430	370–550
****	150–300	200–400
***	80–160	120–250
**	50–120	80–150
*	40–90	70–150

***** Hotels

Amstel, Prof. Tulpplein 1, tel. 22 60 60, 187 B
Amsterdam Apollo, Apollolaan 2, tel. 73 59 22, 445 B
Amsterdam Crest, De Boelelaan 2, tel. 46 23 00. 520 B
Amsterdam Hilton, Apollolaan 138, tel. 78 07 80, 416 B
Amsterdam Marriott, Stadhouderskade 19–21, tel. 83 51 51, 600 B
Amsterdam Sonesta, Kattengat 1, tel. 21 22 23, 700 B
De l'Europe, Nieuwe Doelenstraat 2–8, tel. 23 48 36, 188 B
Garden Hotel, Dijsselhofplantsoen 7, tel. 6 64 21 21, 188 B
Golden Tulip Barbizon Centre, Stadhouderskade 7, tel. 85 13 51, 397 B
Holiday Inn Crowne Plaza, N.Z. Voorburgwal 5, tel. 20 05 00, 361 B
Okura Amsterdam, Ferd. Bolstraat 333, tel. 78 71 11, 502 B
Pulitzer, Prinsengracht 315–331, tel. 22 83 33, 460 B

American, Leidsekade 97, tel. 24 53 22, 331 B

Amsterdam Ascot, Damrak 95–98, tel. 26 00 66, 210 B
Apollofirst, Apollolaan 123, tel. 73 03 33, 72 B
Atlas, Van Eeghenstraat 64, tel. 76 63 36, 46 B
Caransa Crest, Rembrandtplein 19, tel. 22 94 55, 132 B
Damrak, Damrak 49, tel. 26 24 98, 54 B
Delphi, Apollolaan 101–105, tel. 79 51 52, 90 B
De Roode Leeuw, Damrak 93/94, tel. 20 58 75, 135 B
Die Port van Cleve, N.Z. Voorburgwal 178–180, tel. 24 48 60, 193 B
Doelen Crest, Nieuwe Doelenstraat 24, tel. 22 07 22, 159 B
Grand Hotel Krasnapolsky, Dam 9, tel. 5 54 91 11, 600 B
Jolly Hotel Carlton, Vijzelstraat 2–18, tel. 22 22 66, 275 B
Memphis, De Lairessestraat 87, tel. 73 31 41, 150 B
Nicolaas Witsen, Nicolaas Witsenstraat 4, tel. 23 61 43, 58 B
Novotel Amsterdam, Europaboulevard 10, tel. 5 41 11 23, 1093 B
Parkhotel, Stadhouderskade 25, tel. 71 74 74, 360 B
Rembrandt Crest, Herengracht 255, tel. 22 17 27, 215 B
Sander, Jacob Obrechtstraat 69, tel. 6 62 75 74, 36 B
Victoria, Damrak 1–6, tel. 23 42 55, 320 B

Aalborg, Sarphatipark 106–108, tel. 79 90 57, 74 B

Aalders, Jan Luykstraat 13–15, tel. 73 40 27, 53 B
Ambassade, Herengracht 341, tel. 26 23 33, 96 B
AMS Hotel Holland, P. C. Hooftstraat 162, tel. 76 42 53, 137 B
AMS Hotel Museum, P. C. Hooftstraat 2, tel. 83 18 11, 218 B
Arthur Frommer, Noorderstraat 46, tel. 22 03 28, 185 B
Bastion Hotel Amsterdam, Rode Kruisstraat 28, tel. 32 31 31, 90 B
Belfort, Surinameplein 53, tel. 17 43 33, 44 B
Casa 400 (open 1 June–1 October), James Wattstraat 75, tel. 6 65 11 71, 800 B
Cok Tourist Class, Koninginneweg 34–36, tel. 6 64 61 11, 158 B
Cordial, Rokin 62–64, tel. 26 44 11, 92 B
Delta, Damrak 42, tel. 20 26 26, 71 B
Eden, Amstel 144, tel. 26 62 43, 210 B
Estheréa, Singel 303–309, tel. 24 51 46, 153 B
Euromotel Utrechtsebrug, Joan Muyskenweg 10, tel. 6 65 81 81, 261 B
Lancaster, Plantage Middenlaan 48, tel. 20 05 44, 100 B
Maas, Leidsekade 91, tel. 23 38 68, 40 B
Nova, N.Z. Voorburgwal 276, tel. 23 00 66, 134 B
Owl, Roemer Visscherstraat 1, tel. 18 94 84, 63 B
Prins Hendrik, Prins Hendrikkade 53, tel. 23 79 69, 36 B
Roemer Visscher, R. Vissherstraat 10, tel. 12 55 11, 100 B
Slotania, Slotermeerlaan 133, tel. 13 45 68, 175 B
Terminus, Beursstraat 11–19, tel. 23 30 25, 177 B
Toren, Keizersgracht 164, tel. 22 60 33, 90 B
Westropa II, Nassaukade 388–390, tel. 83 49 35, 87 B
Zandbergen, Willemsparkweg 205, tel. 76 93 21, 32 B

Acro, Jan Luykenstraat 44, tel. 6 62 05 26, 120 B

Amsterdam Wiechmann, Prinsengracht 328–330, tel. 26 33 21, 63 B
Armada, Keizersgracht 713–715, tel. 23 29 80, 53 B
Bodeman, Rokin 154–156, tel. 20 15 58, 34 B
Canal House, Keizersgracht 148, tel. 22 51 82, 55 B
City Hotel Amsterdam, Prins Hendrikkade 130, tel. 23 08 36, 49 B
Cynthia, Vondelstraat 44–48, tel. 18 24 28, 100 B

Hotels

De La Poste, Reguliersgracht 3–5, tel. 23 71 05, 38 B
Engeland, Roemer Visscherstraat 30a, tel. 18 08 62, 60 B
Friendship, Van Eeghenstraat 22, tel. 6 64 76 66, 58 B
Groenhof, Vondelstraat 74–78, tel. 16 82 21, 52 B
Imperial, Thorbeckeplein 9, tel. 25 43 08, 37 B
Mikado, Amstel 107–111, tel. 23 70 68, 73 B
Piet Hein, Vossiusstraat 53, tel. 6 62 72 05, 55 B
Prinsen, Vondelstraat 36–38, tel. 16 23 23, 90 B
Rokin, Rokin 73, tel. 26 74 56, 80 B
Savoy, Michelangelostraat 39, tel. 79 03 67, 50 B
Sint Nicolaas, Spuistraat 1a, tel. 26 13 84, 42 B
Smit, P. C. Hooftstraat 24–26, tel. 76 63 43, 118 B
Stadhouder, Stadhouderskade 76, tel. 71 84 28, 48 B
Van Acker, J. W. Brouwersstraat 14, tel. 79 07 45, 24 B
Vondel, Vondelstraat 28–30, tel. 12 01 20, 50 B
Vullings, P. C. Hooftstraat 78, tel. 71 21 09, 24 B
Wilhelmina, Koninginneweg 167–169, tel. 6 62 54 67, 40 B

* Hotels

Abba, Overtoom 122, tel. 18 30 58, 40 B
Acacia, Lindengracht 251, tel. 22 14 60, 26 B
Adolesce, Nieuwe Keizersgracht 26, tel. 26 39 59, 52 B
Albert, Sarphatipark 58, tel. 73 40 83. 31 B
Arsenal, Frans van Mierisstraat 97, tel. 70 22 09, 27 B
Atlanta, Rembrandtplein 8–10, tel. 25 35 85, 68 B
Belga, Hartenstraat 8, tel. 24 90 80, 22 B
De La Haye, Leidsegracht 114, tel. 24 40 44, 40 B
Fantasia, Nieuwe Keizersgracht 16, tel. 24 88 58, 38 B
Galerij, Raadhuisstraat 43, tel. 24 88 51, 20 B
Groenendael, Nieuwendijk 15, tel. 24 48 22, 24 B
Hemony, Hemonystraat 7, tel. 71 42 41, 33 B
Het Witte Huis, Marnixstraat 382, tel. 25 07 77, 38 B
Impala, Leidsekade 77, tel. 23 47 06, 38 B
Interland, Vossiusstraat 46, tel. 6 62 23 44, 55 B
Jupiter, Helmerstraat 14, tel. 18 71 32, 35 B
Kap, Den Texstraat 56, tel. 24 59 08, 32 B
King, Leidsekade 85/86, tel. 24 96 03, 50 B
Linda, Stadhouderskade 131, tel. 6 62 56 68, 40 B
Museumzicht, Jan Luykenstraat 22, 71 29 54, 27 B
P. C. Hooft, P. C. Hooftstraat 63, tel. 6 62 71 07, 40 B
Schirmann, Prins Kendrikkade 23, tel. 24 19 42, 50 B
Seven Bridges, Reguliersgracht 31, tel. 23 13 29, 21 B
Sphinx, Weteringschans 82, tel. 27 36 80, 36 B
Tabu, Marnixstraat 386, tel. 22 75 11, 45 B
The Crown, O.Z. Voorburgwal 21, tel. 26 96 64, 32 B
Titus, Leidsekade 74, tel. 26 57 58, 28 B
Van Haalen, Prinsengracht 520, tel. 26 43 34, 38 B
Van Ostade, Van Ostadestraat 123, tel. 79 34 52, 30 B
Van Rooyen, Helmersstraat 6, tel. 18 45 77, 30 B
Victorie, Victorieplein 42, tel. 73 39 88, 36 B
Vincent van Gogh, Van de Veldestraat 5, tel. 79 60 02, 40 B
Washington, Frans van Mierisstraat 10, tel. 79 67 54, 34 B
Wijnnobel, Vossiusstraat 9, tel. 6 62 22 98, 30 B

For young people

Adam & Eva, Sarphatistraat 105, tel. 24 62 06, 90 B
Bob's Youth Hotel, N.Z. Voorburgwal 92, tel. 23 00 63, 160 B
Cok Student Class, Koningslaan 1, tel. 6 64 61 11, 210 B
Croydon, Warmoesstraat 75, tel. 27 60 65, 22 B
De Filosoof, Anna Vondelstraat 6, tel. 83 30 13, 65 B
Eben Haëzer, Bloemstraat 179, tel. 24 47 17, 114 B
Hans Brinker Stutel, Kerkstraat 136–138, tel. 22 06 87, 255 B

Internationales Centrum, Linnaeusstraat 2c, tel. 92 51 11, 160 B
Kabul, Warmoesstraat 38–42, tel. 23 71 58, 270 B
Keizersgracht, Keizersgracht 15, tel. 25 13 64, 83 B
The Shelter, Barndesteeg 21–25, tel. 25 32 30, 168 B

Information

Netherlands National Tourist Office

Suite 302, 5 Elizabeth Street
Sydney N.S.W. 2000. Tel. 02–276921

Australia

25 Adelaide Street East, Suite 710
Toronto, Ontario M5C 1YC
Tel. 0 (416) 363 1577

Canada

850 Hastings Street, Suite 214
Vancouver, B.S. V6C 1E1
Tel. 0 (604) 684–5720. Telex 04–55133

Union Square (2nd Floor)
Cnr. Plein and Klein Street, P.O. Box 8624
Johannesburg. Tel. 011–236991

South Africa

25–28 Buckingham Gate,
London SW1E 6LD
Tel. 071–630 0451. Telex 269005

United Kingdom

355 Lexington Avenue (21st Floor), New York NY 10017
Tel. 0 (212) 370 7367

United States of America

90 New Montgomery Street, Room 305
San Francisco, CA 94105
Tel. 0 (415) 543 6772

VVV – Tourist Information Centre
Stationsplein 10
NL-1012 AB Amsterdam
Tel. 26 64 44 (information line Mon.–Sat. 9 a.m.–5 p.m.)
Opening times Easter to September: Mon.–Sat. 9 a.m.–11 p.m.,
Sun. 9 a.m.–8 p.m.
Opening times October to Easter: Mon.–Sat. 9 a.m.–6 p.m.,
Sun. 10 a.m.–1 p.m. and 2–5 p.m.

In Amsterdam

VVV – Tourist Information Centre
Leidsestraat 106
Opening times Easter to September: Daily 10.30 a.m.–
5.30 p.m. (9 p.m. in July and August)
Opening times October to Easter: Mon.–Fri. 10.30 a.m.–
5.30 p.m., Sat. 10.30 a.m.–9 p.m.

VVV – Tourist Information Centre
Utrechtseweg A2 (opposite Euromotel)
Opening times Easter to September: Mon.–Sat. 10.30 a.m.–
2 p.m. and 2.30–6.30 p.m.

Opening times and addresses for the VVV tourist information
centres in places described elsewhere in this guide can be
found in "Amsterdam A to Z" under the appropriate heading.

The VVV is the best jumping-off point for tourists since it provides bookings for hotels throughout the Netherlands, as well as theatre and concert reservations, information about cultural events, booking of excursions, canal trips, car rental, etc.

Jazz

See Cafés

Libraries (bibliotheek)

Central Library
Prinsengracht 585, tel. 26 50 65

British Council Library
Keizersgracht 343, tel. 22 36 44

Library for the blind
Molenpad 2, tel. 26 64 65

Amsterdam University Library
Singel 425, tel. 5 25 91 11

Theatre Institute Library
Herengracht 166–68, tel. 23 51 04

Tropical Museum Library
Linnaeusstraat 2, tel. 5 68 82 54

Stedelijk Museum's Art Library
Paulus Potterstraat 13, tel. 73 21 66

Economic History Library
Herengracht 218–20, tel. 24 72 70

International Institute for Social History
Kabelweg 51, tel. 84 36 95

Unesco Centrum Nederland
Oranje Nassaulaan 5, tel. 73 01 00

Kosmos Library
Prins Hendrikkade 142, tel. 26 74 77

Rijksmuseum Library
Stadhouderskade 42, tel. 73 21 21

Maritime Museum Library
Kattenburgerplein 1, tel. 26 22 55

Lost Property (Buro gevonden voorwerpen)

General

Elandsgracht 117 (police station). Tel. 5 59 91 11
Open: Mon. 1–4 p.m., Tues.–Fri. 11 a.m.–4 p.m.

Bicycles

Mastenbroek, Leidsegracht 76. Tel. 23 23 12

Flowers on sale at the Albert Cuyp market

Markets (markten)

See Antiques   Antiques

The Noordermarkt (see below) also has birds for sale.   Birds

Oudemanhuispoort (see Amsterdam A to Z)   Books

Albert Cuypmarkt (see Amsterdam A to Z)   Fabrics, food, clothing, etc.

Dappermarkt (behind the Tropical Museum, see Museums)
Markets Tuesday–Saturday

Noordermarkt (Boerenmarkt), at the Noorderkerk
Market Saturday 10 a.m.–3 p.m.

Ten-Katemarkt (near Kinkerstraat)
Daily market

Vlooienmarkt (see Albert Cuypmarkt, Amsterdam A to Z)   Flea market

Blomenmarkt (see Singel, Amsterdam A to Z)   Flowers

Amstelveld
Markets on Monday mornings from May to October
House plants and garden plants and herbs

N.Z. Voorburgwal   Stamps
Markets Wednesday and Saturday 1–4 p.m.

Motoring Assistance

Automobile Club   ANWB – Koninklijke Nederlandse Toeristenbond (Royal Dutch
                               Tourist Association)
                               Museumplein 5, tel. 73 08 44

Breakdown service   In the event of a breakdown you can ring the ANWB's road
                               patrol, the "wegenwacht", tel. 06 08 88.
                               This service is free of charge if the owner of the vehicle can
                               produce an "international letter of credit" from his or her auto-
                               mobile club. Anyone who is not a member of a motoring orga-
                               nisation affiliated to the AIT (Alliance International de
                               Tourisme) can avail themselves of this service if they take out
                               temporary membership of the ANWB for a month.

State of the road reports   Round-the-clock road reports on weather, traffic conditions,
                               etc. can be obtained by calling the ANWB in the Hague on
                               070/31 31 31.

Museums

Admission prices, museums   The cost of museum admission for adults is between 1 and 8
card   hfl. If you plan to do a lot of sightseeing it's worth buying a
                               museums card. These cost 30 hfl for an adult and can be
                               obtained at one of the museums or from VVV tourist informa-
                               tion centres (see Information). This card gives free admission
                               to many museums in Amsterdam and the rest of the
                               Netherlands.

Museum boat   Many of Amsterdam's museums are right on the canals or
                               quite close to them. From April to September, between 10 a.m.
                               and 5 p.m., there is a special boat service that plies between the
                               landing stage at the VVV information centre at Central Station
                               (see Information) and twelve Amsterdam museums, including
                               the Rijksmuseum, Rembrandthuis and Anne Frank Huis.

Museums   Allard Pierson Museum
                               Oude Turfmarkt 127
                               Open: Tues.–Fri. 10 a.m.–5 p.m.; Sat., Sun., public holidays
                               1–5 p.m.
                               The archaelogical collection of Amsterdam University is one of
                               the biggest university museums of this kind in the world.
                               Ancient Egypt is represented by mummies, sarcophagi, figures
                               of gods and animals, plus collections from the Near East, Meso-
                               potamia, Cyprus and Iran. Ancient Greece and Rome are also
                               well represented.

                               Amstelkring Museum
                               See Amsterdam A to Z, Museum Amstelkring

                               Amsterdams Historisch Museum
                               See Amsterdam A to Z, Amsterdams Historisch Museum

                               Anne Frank Huis
                               See Amsterdam A to Z, Anne Frank Huis

                               Aviodome (National Aeronautics and Space Travel Museum)
                               Schiphol Airport

Open: from April to Oct., Mon–Sun. 10 a.m.–5 p.m.; from Nov. to March, Tues.–Sun. 10 a.m.–5 p.m.

Banketbakkersmuseum
Wibaustraat 220–222
Open: Wed. 10 a.m.–4 p.m.
This museum of baking and pastrymaking has an old bakery with shops, old engravings, recipe books, etc.

Bijbels Museum (Bible museum)
Herengracht 366
Open: Tues.–Sat. 10 a.m.–5 p.m.; Sun., public holidays 1–5 p.m.
The collection, which gives background information on the Bible, is in two fine 18th c. canal mansions. It includes finds from Egypt and Palestine, priceless antique Bibles, and Jewish ritual artefacts. Special exhibitions.

Bilderdijk Museum
de Boelelaan 1105 (in the main building of the Free University)
Open: by prior arrangement (by letter or telephone, tel. 45 43 68).
A collection of drawings, engravings and curios illustrating the life of the Dutch poet Willem Bilderdijk (1756–1831), known for his translations of the classics and patriotic poems and plays.

Bosmuseum
See Amsterdam A to Z, Amsterdamse Bos

Electrische Museum Tramlijn
Haarlemmermeerstation, Amstelveenseweg 264
Open: from April to Oct., Sun. 10 a.m.–6 p.m.
Trips on old trams from Haarlemmermeer Station which, until 1950, was the point of departure for the steam engine to Amstelveen, Aalsmeer and Uithoorn. The old rails were adapted to take trams, and today the museum tram takes visitors into the Amsterdamse Bos and as far as Amstelveen, a stretch of about 6 km/4 miles, making regular use of 15 of the collection of 60 trams, built between 1910 and 1950 in the Netherlands, Germany and Austria. This is a trip particularly enjoyed by children.

Filmmuseum
Vondelpark 3
Open: Mon.–Fri. 10 a.m.–5 p.m.
This museum in a pavilion in the park uses models to recount the history of movie-making supplemented by special exhibitions drawn from foreign film museums. Movie buffs can enjoy screenings of films on particular themes, etc. Plus a large reference library.

Fodor Museum
See Amsterdam A to Z, Keizersgracht

Frederik van Eeden Museum
Singel 425 (University library)
Open: Mon.–Fri. 10 a.m.–1 p.m. and 2–4.30 p.m.
The museum centres on the Dutch writer and social reformer Frederik van Eeden (1860–1932) who in 1898 founded a short-lived community on the lines of his romantic social philosophy.

Geologisch Museum UvA (University of Amsterdam)
Nieuwe Prinsengracht 130
Open: Mon.–Fri. 9 a.m.–5 p.m.
Collection of stones, fossils, minerals, etc.

Historische Verzameling van de Universiteit van Amsterdam
O.Z. Voorburgwal 231
Open: Mon.–Fri. 9 a.m.–5 p.m.
The Historic Collection of posters, books, documents, paint-
ings, etc. illustrates the history of the university since 1632. The
Agnetien Chapel, in which it is housed, has been part of the
university since 1470 and was restored in 1921.

Informatie-Centrum Dienst Ruimtelijke Ordening
(Town Planning Service information centre)
Keizersgracht 440
Open: Tues.–Fri. 12.30–4.30 p.m., Sun. also 6–9 p.m.
A permanent exhibition about the historical development of
Amsterdam. It also gives a full account of the renovation of the
city using charts, drawings, town-plans and slides.

Joods Historisch Museum
(Jewish Historical Museum)
See Amsterdam A to Z, Joods Historisch Museum

Kindermuseum TM Junior
See Amsterdam A to Z, Tropenmuseum

Madame Tussaud's Panopticum
See Amsterdam A to Z, Kalverstraat

Multatuli Museum
Korsjespoortsteeg 20
Open: Tues. 10 a.m.–5 p.m. (and by appointment, tel. 24 74 27)
Exhibition commemorating the Dutch writer Multatuli, whose
real name was Eduard Douwes Dekker (1820–1887), and who in
his free-thinking, humanitarian novels (including "Max Have-
laar or The Dutch on Java"), sharply attacked the Dutch colonial
system.

Museum Amstelkring
See Amsterdam A to Z, Museum Amstelkring

Museum Fodor
See Amsterdam A to Z, Keizersgracht

Museum Overholland
Museumplein 4
Open: Tues.–Sat. 11 a.m.–5 p.m.; Sun., public holidays
1–5 p.m.
The Museum Overholland has been housed since 1987 in a
building built in 1925 in the style of American architect Frank
Lloyd Wright. Its theme is "Art on paper since 1970" and it has a
collection of drawings, watercolours, gouaches, etc.

Museum Van Loon
See Amsterdam A to Z, Keizersgracht

Museum Willet Holthuysen
Herengracht 605

Open: Tues.–Sun. 11 a.m.–5 p.m.
A typical 17th c. patrician house, which has been made into a museum, on the Herengracht (see Amsterdam A to Z, Herengracht), with an 18th c. garden.
Temporary exhibitions.

Nederlands Centrum voor Ambachten
(Netherlands crafts centre)
Nieuwendijk 16
Open: Mon.–Sun. 10 a.m.–5 p.m. (closed Wed. in Feb., Mar. and Nov.)
Here it is still possible to see demonstrations of crafts such as cheese-making, glass-blowing, making clogs, pewter work, lead glazing, painting Delft china, pottery, silver-working, spinning and weaving.

NINT (Dutch Institute for Industry and Technology)
Tolstraat 129
Open: Mon.–Fri. 10 a.m.–4 p.m.; Sat., Sun., public holidays 1–5 p.m.
The exhibition is designed to familiarise the visitor with various aspects of modern technology (energy, photography, communications, etc.).

Persmuseum (press museum)
Cruquiusweg 31
Open: Mon.–Fri. 11 a.m.–5 p.m.
The press museum has a collection of newspapers, magazines, posters, pamphlets and cartoons dating back to the early 17th c. Temporary exhibitions.

Peter Stuyvesant Stichting
Drentsestraat 21
Open: Mon.–Fri. 9 a.m.–noon and 1–4 p.m.
Viewing of modern painting and sculpture intended for business and public art uses.

Planetarium
Kromwijkdreef 11
Open: Wed. 12.30–5.30 p.m.; Sat., Sun. 9.30 a.m. 5.30 p.m.

Rembrandthuis
See Amsterdam A to Z, Rembrandthuis

Rijksmuseum
See Amsterdam A to Z, Rijksmuseum

Scheepvaartmuseum (maritime museum)
Kattenburgerplein 1
Open: Tues.–Sat. 10 a.m.–5 p.m.; Sun., public holidays 1–5 p.m.
Collection of model ships, globes, navigation instruments and pictures on a maritime theme.

Schriftmuseum J.A.Dortmond
Singel 425 (university library)
Open: Mon.–Fri. 10 a.m.–1 p.m. and 2–4.30 p.m.
The museum, named after the collector J. A. Dortmond, illustrates the development of the art of writing from about 3000 B.C. to the present day. The handwriting department contains documentation on the art of writing.

Museums

Six Collectie
Amstel 218
Access only by letter of introduction from the Rijksmuseum
(see Amsterdam A to Z, Rijksmuseum)
Private collection of 17th c. Dutch masters, including
Rembrandt.

Spaarpottenmuseum (museum of money boxes)
Raadhuisstraat 12
Open: Mon.–Fri. 1–4 p.m.
Collection of more than 12,000 money boxes from all over the
world.

Stedelijk Museum
See Amsterdam A to Z, Stedelijk Museum

Theatermuseum
Herengracht 168
Open: Tues.–Sun. 11 a.m.–5 p.m.
The theatre museum, which forms part of the Theatre Institute,
presents the history of the Dutch theatre in drawings, sculpture, paintings, posters, props, etc. The Theatre Institute occu-
pies five magnificent houses on the Herengracht, and their
architecture and furnishings warrant a visit on their own
account. Temporary exhibitions.

Tropenmuseum
See Amsterdam A to Z, Tropenmuseum

Van Gogh Museum
See Amsterdam A to Z, Van Gogh Museum

Verzetsmuseum Amsterdam (Museum of the Resistance)
Lekstraat 63
Open: Tues.–Fri. 10 a.m.–5 p.m., Sat., Sun., public holidays 1–
5 p.m.
Museum of the Netherlands Resistance movement during the
German Occupation from 1940 to 1945, housed in a former
Jewish synagogue.

Werft 't Kromhout (shipyard museum)
Hoogte Kadijk 147
Open: Mon.–Fri. 10 a.m.–4 p.m.
Permanent exhibition of shipyard machinery, models and ship-
wrights' tools, plus some old ships at their moorings.

Zoological Museum
See Amsterdam A to Z, Artis

**Museums concerned with
land reclamation**

Delta Expo
Burgh-Haamsteda
Open: from April to Oct., Mon.–Sun. 10 a.m.–5 p.m.; from Nov.
to March, Wed.–Sat. 10 a.m.–5 p.m.
The Delta Expo, on the Neeltje Jans island in the Oosterschelde
(accessible by motorway), is concerned with the construction
of the world's biggest flood barrier across the 9 km/5.6 mile
width of the estuary of the Oosterscheld (eastern arm of the
River Scheld); from April to October a visit to the exhibition is
done in conjunction with a boat-trip along the flood barrier.

Zuiderzeemuseum
Wierdijk 18, Enkhuizen

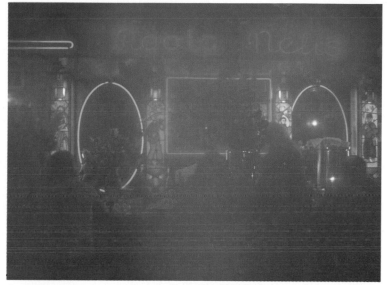

Bar in Amsterdam

On the Walletjes – the red light district (see Amsterdam A–Z)

Open: from mid-April to mid-October, daily 10 a.m.–
5 p.m.
Open-air museum

Nightlife

Amsterdam's nightlife centres on three areas. The oldest is
around the port, in Nieuwendijk and Zeedijk (see Amsterdam
A to Z, Walletjes). The nearby Rembrandtsplein and Thorbeckeplein are full of clubs – the Thorbeckeplein has a bar,
nightclub or cabaret in virtually every one of its buildings. Here
the floorshows are mostly striptease acts. The third and newest
centre for nightlife is in and around the Leidseplein, where
there are quite a few discotheques as well. Hotel bars are also a
favourite haunt for real nightowls.

Bars

Apollo (Apollo Hotel), Apollolaan 2, tel. 73 59 22
Brainbox Bar, Station Building Schiphol Airport, tel. 15 21 50
Canal Bar (Okura Hotel), Ferd. Bolstraat 333, tel. 78 71 11
Continental Bodega, Lijnbaansgracht 246, tel. 23 90 98
Halfmoon Bar (Amsterdam Hilton), Apollolaan 138, tel. 78 07 80
Library Bar (Mariott Hotel), Stadhouderskade 19–21,
tel. 83 51 51
O'Henry's, Rokin 89, tel. 25 14 98
Palmbar (Hotel Krasnapolsky), Dam 9, tel. 5 54 91 11
Pianobar Focus, O.Z. Voorburgwal 189, tel.27 18 34
Sherrycan, Spui 30, tel. 26 12 55
Tasmanbar (Victoria Hotel), Damrak 1–6, tel. 23 42 55
The Old Bell, Rembrandtsplein 46, tel. 24 76 28
U.B.Q., P. C. Hooftstraat 100, tel. 79 20 04

Bars with live music

Alto, Korte Leidsedwarsstraat 115, tel. 26 32 49
Amstel Hotel Bar, Prof. Tulpplein 1, tel. 22 60 60
Bamboo Bar, Lange Leidsedwarsstraat 64, tel. 24 39 93
Cab Kaye's Jazz Piano Bar, Beulingsraat 9, tel. 23 35 94
Clock Bar (Crest Hotel), De Boelelaan 2, tel. 42 98 55
Joseph Lam Jazzclub, v. Diemenstraat 8, tel. 22 80 86
Pianobar Le Maxim, Leidsekruisstraat 35, tel. 24 19 20
The String, Nes 98, tel. 25 90 15

Taster bars

See entry

Discotheques

Boston Club (Sonesta Hotel), Kattengat 1, tel. 24 55 61
De Schakel, Korte Leidsedwarsstraat 49, tel. 22 76 85
Juliana's, Apollolaan 138–140, tel. 73 73 13
Mazzo, Rozengracht 114, tel. 26 75 00
'T Okshoofd, Herengracht 114, tel. 22 76 85
Zorba de Buddha Rajneesh, O.Z. Voorburgwal 216, tel. 25 96 42

Sex shows

Topless bars, striptease and sex shows can be found around
the Rembrandtsplein and Leidseplein, or in the Walletjes, the
red light district.

Opening Times

Banks

Mon.–Fri. 9 a.m.–4 p.m.

Chemists

Mon.–Sat. 8 a.m.–5.30 p.m.

Many churches are only open during services. At other times the verger should be contacted.	Churches
Opening times are the same as for other shops. They stay open in the lunch-hour but are usually closed on Monday mornings.	Department stores
Mon.–Fri. 9 a.m.–5 p.m.	Post offices
Shops are usually open from 9 a.m. to 6 p.m. during the week and until 5 p.m. on Saturdays. On Thursdays most stay open late until 9 p.m. They usually close in the lunch-hour, as well as closing for a morning or an afternoon or even a whole day once a week.	Shops

Parks

Amsterdamse Bos
See Amsterdam A to Z, Amsterdamse Bos.

Beatrixpark
next to the RAI congress centre

Erasmuspark
on the Jan van Galenstraat

Hortus Botanicus UVA (Botanic Garden of Amsterdam University)
See Amsterdam A to Z Hortus Botanicus

Hortus Botanicus VU (Botanic Garden of the Free University)
Van der Boechorststraat
Open: Mon.–Fri. 8 a.m.–4.15 p.m.
Admission free

Julianapark
Prins Bernhardplein

Oosterpark
near the Singelgracht

Rembrandtspark
on the Einsteinweg (A10)

Vondelpark
See Amsterdam A to Z, Vondelpark

Westerpark
on the Haarlemmervaart

Pawnbroker (pandjeshuis)

Oudezijds Voorburgwal 300, tel. 22 24 21	Municipal pawnbroker

Petrol

The only leaded petrol available in the Netherlands is "Super", or four star, and that, too, is also obtainable unleaded.

Pets

Cats and dogs

Anyone wanting to take their cat or dog into the Netherlands must have an official veterinary certificate of vaccination against rabies for their animal. The vaccination must have taken place at least 30 days before entry and for a dog must be valid for a year and for a cat valid for six months.

Police (politie)

Police headquarters

Elandsgracht 117, tel. 5 56 91 11

Emergency number

To call the police in an emergency dial 22 22 22, day or night.

Post, telegraph and telephone

Main post office

Nieuwezijds Voorburgwal 182, tel. 5 55 89 11
Open: Mon.–Wed., Fri. 8.30 a.m.–6 p.m., Thurs. 8.30 a.m.–8.30 p.m., Sat. 9 a.m.–noon
Open daily round the clock for long-distance phone calls and telegrams. Entrance at back of building.

Parcel post

Post office at Oosterdokskade 5
Open: Mon.–Fri. 8.30 a.m.–9 p.m., Sat. 9 a.m.–noon

Opening times

The other Amsterdam post offices are open from Monday to Friday between 9 a.m. and 5 p.m.

Postal rates

The postal rates within the Netherlands also apply to anywhere inside the European Community.

postcards
Netherlands: 0.55 hfl
abroad: 0.65 hfl

letters
Netherlands: 0.75 hfl
abroad: 0.90 hfl

International direct dialling

International calls can be made from public phone booths and from post offices. To call internationally direct from a public phone you need to put in at least 25 cents, wait for the dial tone, then dial the international code (09) and wait for the dial tone again. As soon as you hear this go ahead and dial the code for the country immediately followed by the area code (minus the first 0) and the subscriber's number.

International enquiries

Tel. 00 18

Country codes for
international direct dialling

From the Netherlands:	Australia	61
	Canada	1
	South Africa	27
	United Kingdom	44
	United States	1
To the Netherlands:		31

Programme of events

The VVV publishes a weekly news-sheet in English called "Amsterdam This Week" which gives details of what's on and

is obtainable from VVV tourist information centres and the big hotels.
The Dutch "What's On" publications are "Aktueel Amsterdam" (from bookshops) and "Amsterdam Uitkrant" (monthly from the Stadschouwburg).

Public Holidays/Commemorations

New Year, Good Friday (most shops are open), Easter, the Queen's Birthday (30 April), Ascension Day, Whitsun, Christmas.

Public Holidays

4 May (for the victims of the Second World War, not a public holiday), 5 May (Liberation day; most shops are open).

Commemorations

Public Transport

Amsterdam is covered by a very good public transport network. Most people travel by bus or tram. The building of the Underground system, the Metro, was halted by massive public protest because of its feared environmental impact, but it does have two lines and 20 stations.
The buses, trams and Metro run until midnight when night-buses take over.

Bus, Tram, Metro

All public transport fares and timetables are co-ordinated by the City of Amsterdam, through its municipal public transport subsidiary, the GVB (Gemeentevervoerbedrijf). The city is divided up into zones with separate tariffs. The fare depends on whether the journey is through one, two or three zones. The location of the zones is shown at the various public transport stops.

Co-ordinated City Transport

There are no single tickets, only strip tickets (strippenkaart). Once you've worked out from the zone plan which zone your destination is in you get your strip ticket cancelled accordingly by the conductor or automatic ticket machine. The smallest "strippenkaart" is good for two trips within the centre by bus, tram or Metro, or one trip through two zones. There are also tickets with 3, 10 or 15 "strippen".
The ticket can be used for more than one person if it has enough "strippen".

Strip tickets

For visitors it's much easier to buy a day ticket. This entitles you to a whole day and night's travel on all tram, bus and Metro lines.

Day tickets

Since parking problems, theft, etc. mean it is always better to leave the car behind when in Amsterdam and take to public transport, it is a good idea for a longer stay to buy a ticket for two, three or more days.

Tickets for 2, 3 or more days

You can also buy a 60-minute ticket from conductors on trams and buses.

60-minute ticket

Since the public transport system throughout the whole of the Netherlands is divided into zones and all transport undertak-

National strip-ticket

ings operate the same tariff per zone, for longer excursions it makes sense to buy the "nationale strippenkaart" which can be used on all Dutch bus, tram and Metro lines.
The 15-strip ticket must be bought in advance, and is obtainable from stations, post offices, VVV offices, and transport operators.

Ticket sales

Day and strip tickets can be obtained from all tram and bus drivers and the Metro stations have automatic strip ticket dispensers. These, as well as the multi-day tickets, can also be bought at the GVB information and sales point in front of the central station and the Bulldog Café on the Leidseplein.

Information

Detailed information on all aspects of public transport can be obtained at the GVB information and sales point in front of the central station (open: Mon.–Fri. 7 a.m.–10.30 p.m.; Sat., Sun. 8 a.m.–10.30 p.m.) and in the Bulldog Café on the Leidseplein (open: Mon.–Fri. 8 a.m.–9.30 p.m.; Sat., Sun. 10 a.m.–5 p.m.). By phone: 27 27 27 (from 7 a.m.–11 p.m.).
A free "welcome" leaflet with useful information on public transport and a city plan is available in hotels or at the GVB information points mentioned, at the GVB counter in the Amstel Station and the GVB head office (Prins Hendrikkade 108–110).

Radio/Television

In line with the Dutch attitude that everyone should be free to express themselves, radio and television is in the hands of a number of private stations who put together widely differing programmes reflecting their religious or political views.
These Radio/TV associations are funded by their members' contributions which also influence the amount of time the stations get on the air. There are, among others, Protestant (EO), Catholic (KRO) and Socialist (VARA) stations as well as the independent state-financed Nederlandse Omroep Stichting with its headquarters in Hilversum.

Restaurants

In terms of the minimum price for a menu Amsterdam restaurants can roughly be divided into the following categories:

Higher priced (over 50 hfl)
Medium priced (30–50 hfl)
Lower priced (18–30 hfl)

Higher priced

Brasserie van Baerle
Van Baerlestraat 158, tel. 79 15 32
Closed Sat.

Ciel Bleu (Okura Hotel, French cuisine)
Ferd. Bolstraat 333, tel. 78 71 11

De Cost gaet voor de Baet uyt
(French cuisine)
Oudebrugsteeg 16, tel. 24 70 50

De Goudsbloem (Hotel Pulitzer, French cuisine)
Reestraat 8, tel. 25 38 88

De Kersentuin (Garden Hotel)
Dijsselhofplantsoen 7, tel. 6 64 21 21
Closed Sun.

D'Vijff Vlieghen
Vliegendesteeg 1, tel. 24 83 69

Excelsior (Hotel de l'Europe)
Nieuwe Doelenstraat 2–4, tel. 23 48 36

La Rive (Amstel Hotel, French cuisine)
Prof. Tulpplein 1, tel. 22 60 60
(evenings only)

Le Reflet d'Or (Grand Hotel Krasnapolsky)
Dam 9, tel. 5 54 91 11

Les Quatre Canetons
Prinsengracht 1111, tel. 24 63 07
Closed Sun.

Mart Inn (restaurant on the port)
De Ruyterkade 7, tel. 25 62 77

Rib Room Restaurant
(Sonesta Hotel, French cuisine)
Kattengat 1, tel. 21 22 23

Rosarium
Amstelpark 1, tel. 44 40 85
Closed Sun.

Bistro La Forge (French cuisine)   Medium priced
Korte Leidsedwarsstraat 26, tel. 24 00 95

De Groene Lanteerne
Harlemmerstraat 43, tel. 24 19 52
Closed Mon., Sun.

De Kelderhof
Prinsengracht 494, tel. 22 06 82

De Nachtwacht
Thorbeckeplein 2, tel. 22 47 94

Haesje Claes
N.Z. Voorburgwal 320, tel. 24 99 98

Henri Smits (French cuisine)
Beethovenstraat 55, tel. 79 17 06

La Belle Epoque (French cuisine)
Leidseplein 14, tel. 23 83 61

Mangerie (French cuisine)
Spuistraat 3b, tel. 25 22 18

Miranda Paviljoen
Amsteldijk 223, tel. 44 88 19

Restaurants

'T Heertje
Herenstraat 16, tel. 25 81 27
Closed Wed.

Lower priced   De Bak
Prinsengracht 193, tel. 25 79 72

De Boemerang
Weteringschans 171, tel. 23 42 51
Closed Wed.

Dirck Dirckz
Bilderdijkstraat 102–106, tel. 18 31 76

Hollands Glorie
Kerkstraat 220–222, tel. 24 47 64

Sing Singel
Singel 101, tel. 25 25 81

Smits Koffiehuis
Stationsplein 10, tel. 23 37 77

Talk Small
Willemsparkweg 1–3, tel. 6 62 00 29

Tourist menu   Restaurants displaying the "Tourist Menu" sign offer a three-course menu for 19.50 hfl (current price).

David en Goliath
Kalverstraat 92, tel. 23 67 36

De Gerstekorrel (in hotel of same name)
Damstraat 22–24, tel. 24 97 71

Heineken Hoeg
Kleine Gartmanplantsoen 1–3, tel. 23 07 00

Oud Holland
N.Z. Voorburgwal 105, tel. 24 68 48

Simon Restaurant
Spuistraat 299, tel. 23 11 41

Neerlands Dis   Restaurants with the "Neerlands Dis" logo serve Dutch specialities.

Bodega Keyzer
Van Baerlestraat 96, tel. 71 14 41
Closed Sun.

De Rooede Leeuw (in hotel of same name)
Damrak 93/94, tel. 20 58 75

Poort Restaurant
(Hotel Die Port van Cleve)
N.Z. Voorbugwal 178–180, tel. 24 00 47

Fish restaurants   Albatros Seafood House
Westerstraat 264, tel. 27 99 32
Closed Sun.

De Oesterbar
Leidseplein 10, tel. 23 29 88

Le Pêcheur
Regulierdwarsstraat 32, tel. 24 31 21

Lucius
Spuistraat 247, tel. 24 18 31
(evenings only)

Sluizer
Utrechtsestraat 43–45, tel. 26 35 57

Le Cercle (Casino Amsterdam)   Late-night
Apollolaan 138–140, tel. 6 64 99 11

Baldur   Vegetarian
Weteringschans 76, tel. 24 46 72
Closed Sun.

De Waaghals
Frans Halsstraat 29, tel. 79 96 09
Closed Mon.

China Corner   Chinese
Damstraat 1, tel. 22 88 16

Dynasty
Reguliersdwarsstraat 30, tel. 26 84 00
Closed Tues. (higher priced)

Bali   Indonesian
Leidsestraat 95, tel. 22 78 78
Closed Sun.

Sama Sebo
P.C. Hooftstraat 27, tel. 6 62 81 46
Closed Sun.

Speciaal
Nieuwe Leliestraat 142, tel. 24 97 06

Isola Bella   Italian
Thorbeckeplein 7, tel. 26 95 02

La Cantina
Rokin 87, tel. 25 89 45

Kei   Japanese
Apollolaan 138–140, tel. 78 07 80

Teppan Yaki Steakhouse
(Okura Hotel)
Ferd. Bolstraat 333, tel. 78 71 11

Rum Runners   Caribbean
Prinsengracht 277, tel. 27 40 79

Rose's Cantina   Mexican
Reguliersdwarsstraat 38, tel. 25 97 97

Russian	Moscow
	Herengracht 561, tel. 23 43 71

Shopping

Shopping streets	The P. C. Hooftstraat is where you'll find all sorts of upmarket shops, especially exclusive boutiques. The Kalverstraat is particularly well supplied with shoe-shops. For second-hand shops, collector items and junkshops the place to go is the Jordaan, the area between the Prinsengracht and the Lijnbaansgracht.
Antiques	See entry
Ballet, theatrical items	Le Papillon, Rokin 104
Books	See Bookshops
Camping gear	Gaasper Camping, Loosdrechtsedreef 7 Neef Sport, Raadhuisstraat 32
Cheese	Abraham Kef, Marnixstraat 192 De Ark, Jacob van Campenstraat 35
Chemists	Jacob Hooij & Co, Kloveniersburgwal 12 (old-fashioned chemist's shop) B. Heinhuis, Spuistraat 58 Marjo, Zeedijk 68 Tijhuis, Claas van Maarssenplein 37
Clogs (klompen)	't Klompenhuisje, Nieuwe Hoogstraat 917 (open: 11 a.m.–6 p.m. daily) De Klompenboer, N.Z. Voorburgwal 20 Clockwitz, Herengracht 305 A. W. G. Otten, Albert Cuypstraat 102
Coffee roasting	Geels en Co., Warmoesstraat 67
Cosmetics	De Driehoek, Martelaarsgracht 18 Duffels, International Cosmetics, Buitenveldertselaan 36
Delft porcelain, crystal and chinoiserie	Focke & Meltzer, Kalverstraat 176 Van Gelder, Van Baerlestraat 40 Kado Boutique Exclusive, Hoofweg 478 Het Kristalhuis, Rozenboomsteeg 12–14 Porcella, Hugo de Vrieslaan 45 Rosenthal Studio House, Heiligeweg 49–51 Wille & Co., Nieuwendijk 216–218
Delicatessen	Dikker & Thijs, Leidsestraat 82
Department stores	See entry
Herbs	Herb shop, Kloveniersburgwal 12
Jewellers	Schaap en Citroen, Kalverstraat 1 and Rokin 12 Bernard Schipper, Kalverstraat 36–38 Elka Watch, Kalverstraat 206 Smit Ouwekerk, Singel 320 Hans Appenzeller, Grimburgwal 1

Amstel Diamonds, Amstel 208	Jewellers with
Diamonds Direct Herman Schipper B.V., Heiligeweg 3	diamond-cutting
The Mill Diamonds, Rokin 123	
Willem van Pampus Diamond Center, Kalverstraat 117	

Brigitte's Boutique, Amstel 328	Kitchenware
Metz & Co., Keizersgracht 455	

Het Kantenhuis, Kalverstraat 124	Linen
See entry	Markets
See entry	Opening times
André Coppenhagen, Bloemgracht 38	Pearls
Cards for Days, Huidenstraat	Postcards

Portobello Giftshop, Rokin 107	Souvenirs
Rally Wachtel, Damstraat 6	
Rozengalerie, Rozengracht 75	
De Voetboog art, Voetboogsteeg 16	
A. Smit, Buikslotermeerplein 254	
The Turquoise Tomahawk, Berenstraat 16	

P. C. G. Hajenius, Rokin 92 (Purveyor to the Royal Household)	Tobacconists
A. M. van Lookeren, Beethovenstraat 88	
J. van Beek, Nieuwendijk 109	
J. Naarden, Damstraat 2a	

Witte Tandenwinkel, Runstraat	Toothbrushes

van der Linden	Foodstores open at night
Korte Koningstraat 7	

Open: Mon.–Sat. 4 p.m.–1 a.m., Sun. 2 p.m.–1 a.m.
Harms
Zeedijk 83
Open: Mon.–Sat. 6 p.m.–midnight, Sun. 8 p.m.–midnight

Reitema
2e Rozendwarsstraat 9
Open: Tues.–Fri. 4 p.m.–1 a.m., Sat. 1 p.m.–1 a.m., Sun.
6 p.m.–1 a.m.

Nightshop
Stationsweg 316
Open: 4 p.m.–1 a.m. daily

Focke Groot
Overtoom 478
Open: 4 p.m.–1 a.m. daily

Gerritse
van Woustraat 243
Open: Mon.–Sat. 4 p.m.–1 a.m., Sun. 5 p.m.–midnight

Sightseeing trips

Nearly everyone goes on a canal trip when they're in Amsterdam – there are over 65 glass-topped boats taking visitors	Canal trips

Sightseeing trips

Boat trip on the canals

through the canals and out onto the Amstel and round the harbour.

It's also quite an experience to do the tour at night, especially the candlelit version, on a boat lit by candles with wine and cheese included in the price.

The tours depart every hour during the summer, and at longer intervals in winter. They last between an hour and half a day, and the commentary is in four languages.

Tours can be booked in the Amsterdam VVV tourist information centres, or with the operators direct. Reduced price tickets are obtainable in youth hostels.

Operators

Reederei Lovers B.V.
Prins Hendrikkade 25–27
opposite central station, tel. 22 21 81 or 25 93 23

Holland International
opposite central station, tel. 22 77 88

Reederei Noord-Zuid
Stadhouderskade 25, tel. 79 13 70

Reederei Kooij
Rokin on the Spui, tel. 23 38 10 or 23 41 86

Reederei Plas
Damrak at the station, tel. 24 54 06 or 22 60 96

Bus trips

Trips in and around Amsterdam can be booked with the following operators (or in the VVV tourist information centres):

Holland International Travel Group, Rokin 54, tel. 26 44 66
Holland Travel Service, Rokin 9, tel. 23 43 90
Key Tours, Dam 19, tel. 24 73 10
Lindbergh Travel Bureau, Damrak 26, tel. 22 27 66

Excursions outside Amsterdam include trips to the fishing villages of Marken and Volendam, the cheese market at Alkmaar,
the tulip fields of the Keukenhof, The Hague, Delft, and the
Zuiderzee (see entries in Amsterdam A to Z).

KLM, the Dutch airline (tel. 74 77 47), operates half-hour flights
over Amsterdam on Saturdays from April to October.

Sightseeing from the air

Sightseeing itineraries

The following itineraries are intended for anyone who only has
a short time to spend in Amsterdam. They pick out the highlights so that you can make the most of your visit. **Bold** print
indicates the relevant headings in Amsterdam A to Z.

To get a general impression of the city's highlights, and some
kind of feel for that special Amsterdam atmosphere, the first
thing to do is go for a walk round the city centre, starting from
the central station (**Centraal Spoorweg Station**). Go south
down the busy Damrak to the **Dam**, with the national monument, the **Koninklijk Paleis** and the **Nieuwe Kerk**. Get swept up
in the hustle and bustle of the **Kalverstraat**, before pausing for a
while in the **Amsterdams Historisch Museum** and the **Begijnhof**. Make for the southern end of the Kalverstraat and the
Munt tower (see **Muntplein**), then close by you have the flower
market on the **Singel**. Turn eastward along the Reguliersbreestraat to the **Rembrandtsplein** and from there via Amstelstraat
and the Blauwbrug (view of the **Magere Brug**) cross to the
Waterlooplein (see **Jodenbuurt**), where Amsterdam's famous
fleamarket, the Vlooienmarkt, is held. Here you can see the new
musical theatre, "Het Muziektheater" (see **Stopera**), the **Mozes
en Aaronkerk**, and the **Rembrandthuis**. Turning north along the
Sint Antoniesbreestraat you pass the **Zuiderkerk** before reach-
ing the **Waaggebouw** on the **Nieuwmarkt**. Passing through the
middle of the **Walletjes**, Amsterdam's redlight district, taking a
turn along the **Achterburgwal** and perhaps detouring to the
Oude Kerk, you arrive back at Centraal Station again.
If you don't devote the whole day to walking round the centre or
spend a long while at individual places, a museum visit can be
fitted into the afternoon. Whether it is to the **Rijksmuseum,
Stedelijk Museum** or **Van Gogh Museum** depends on your
particular taste, but since all three museums are quite close
together on the south-western edge of the inner city canal
district it is possible to combine visits to more than one
museum.
Undoubtedly the grand finale to a visit to Amsterdam is a boat
trip on the canals (see above, Sightseeing), which also takes in
the port (see **Haven**). If time is short this can be postponed to
the evening when the bridges and the magnificent houses
along the canals are illuminated, an experience that will serve
to confirm that the best way to get to know Amsterdam is from
the peace and quiet of her waterways.

One day

If two days are available to spend in Amsterdam the one-day
itinerary can be used but with more time spent on getting to

Two days

know some places better. In the morning, for example, you could visit one of the art museums, the Jewish Historical Museum (see **Joods Historisch Museum**) or the **Anne Frank Huis**. If you opt for the latter this could be combined with a visit to the nearby **Westerkerk** and a stroll along the **Herengracht** in the western part of the old city.

In the afternoon a visit to a diamond cutting centre is highly recommended (see above, Diamond Cutting). And a trip on a canal bike (see above, Canal bikes) is another way of getting to know Amsterdam from the water, this time under your own steam.

Three days

Besides letting you get to know the city better a longer stay also gives you time to take trips to some of the places worth visiting not far from Amsterdam. If the tulips are in bloom a visit to the **Keukenhof** is virtually a must. At other times of year, however, it is worth going via **Monnickendam** and **Marken** to **Edam** and **Volendam**, which like Marken is famous for its traditional costumes, and perhaps carry on to **Hoorn**, with its picturesque old buildings. Other options are a day-trip via **Aalsmeer**, where the daily flower auctions are held, and the ancient university town of **Leiden**, to **Delft**, with its old town ringed by canals, or perhaps a visit to the open-air museum of **Zaanse Schans**.

Sport

Football	Ajax-Stadion, Middenweg Olympia-Stadion, Stadionplein
Bowling	Bowling Centre Knijn, Scheldeplein 3
Golf	Golfclub Olympus, Jan Vroegopsingel
Miniature Golf	There are miniature golf courses in the Amstelpark, the Amsterdamse Bos and the Sloterpark
Skating	Jaap Edenbaan Radioweg 64 Open: Oct.–March.
Tennis	Frans Ottenstadion Stadionstraat 10
Swimming	See Swimming Pools
Riding	Amsterdamse Manege, Amsterdamse Bos
Rowing	Jachthaven Neptunus, Amsterdamse Bos Rowing boats for hire
Sailing	Jachthaven Waterlust, Amsterdamse Bos Sailing boats for hire

Stations (Stationen)

Central Station	Amsterdam's Central Station (see Amsterdam A to Z, Centraal Spoorweg Station) is the hub of the local and long-distance communications network.

Taster bars usually have china taps

Amstel Station, Julianaplein
Muiderport Station, Oosterpoortplein
Amsterdam RAI, Europaboulevard
Amsterdam Zuid, World Trade Center

Other stations

Tel. 20 22 66
Mon.–Fri. 8 a.m.–10 p.m., Sat., Sun., public holidays 9 a.m.–
10 p.m.

Train enquiries

Swimming

Bredius, Spaarndammerdijk
Flevopark, Zeeburgerdijk 230
Florapark, Sneeuwbalstraat 5
Jan van Galen, Jan van Galenstraat 315
Mirandabad, De Mirandalaan 9
Sloterparkbad, Slotermeerlaan 2

Outdoor pools

Florapark, Sneeuwbalstraat 5
Heiligeweg, Heiligeweg 19
Marnixbad, Marnixplein 9
Mirandabad (inc. wave action), De Mirandalaan 9
Sloterparkbad, Slotermeerlaan 2

Indoor pools

Andreas Bonnstraat 28
Marnixplein 9
Da Costakade 200
Le Sweelinckstraat 10

Bath-houses

127

Taster bars

Taster bars, where the main drinks served are brandy and liqueurs, are an Amsterdam speciality. In some what you get is often not a ready-made tipple but a concoction mixed to that particular bar's own recipe. The glass will be filled so full that you have to get down and bend right over it to take the first sip. Otherwise you run the risk, however steady your hand, of spilling some of that precious liquid!

Bols Taverne, Rozengracht 106, tel. 24 57 52
De Drie Fleschjes, Gravenstraat 18, tel. 24 84 43
Hooghoudt, Reguliersgracht 11, tel. 25 50 30
Wijnand Fockinck, Pijlsteeg 31, tel. 24 39 89

All these taster bars take the day off on Sundays!

Taxis

Phone numbers

Dial 77 77 77 to order a taxi. Some ranks can also be dialled direct:

Dam, tel. 5 70 42 01
Central Station, tel. 5 70 42 00
Nieuwmarkt, tel. 5 70 42 05
Westermarkt, tel. 5 70 42 08

Fares

The fare is made up of a basic rate plus the rate for the distance covered, plus supplements for night-work, etc. The fare includes the tip, but the driver will certainly not object if it is rounded up to the nearest guilder.

Water taxis

See entry

Telephone, telegraph

See Post, telegraph and telephone

Theatres, concert halls

Theatres

Amsterdams Marionettentheater
Brouwersgracht 51, tel. 26 49 83

Bellevue
Leidsekade 90, tel. 24 72 48
Opera and ballet

Theater de Brakke Grond
Nes 53–55, tel. 24 03 94
Also performances in English

Theater Carré
Amstel 115–125, tel. 22 52 25
Amsterdam's biggest theatre for plays, cabaret, musicals and dance (no fixed programme)

Cleyntheater (Nieuwendam)
H. Cleyndertweg 63a, tel. 37 18 15

Theater de Engelenbak
Nes 71, tel. 26 36 44 and 23 57 23

Het Muziektheater
Waterlooplein
Opera and ballet

De Kleine Komedie
Amstel 55–58, tel. 24 05 34

Lilalo Jiddish Cabaret
De Clercqstraat 109, tel. 18 00 71

De Meervaart
Osdorpplein 67, tel. 10 73 93

Mickery
Rozengracht 117, tel. 23 67 77
Experimental theatre with foreign company

Nieuwe de la Mar Theater
Marnixstraat 404, tel. 23 34 62

De Populier
Nieuwe Herengracht 93, tel. 23 36 73

Shaffy Theater
Keizersgracht 324, tel. 23 13 11

Stadschouwburg
Leidseplein 26, tel. 24 23 11
Amsterdam's most beautiful theatre; mainly drama, but also
opera and ballet

Theater de Suikerhof
Prinsengracht 381, tel. 22 75 71

Theater Tingel Tangel
Nieuwezijds Voorburgwal 282, tel. 26 46 95

Amstelveens Poppentheater   Children's theatre
Wolfert van Borsselenweg 85a, tel. 45 04 39

Diridas Poppentheater
Hobbemakade 68, tel. 62 15 88

Poppentheater Musquit
Rechtsboomsloot 42, tel. 26 40 15

De Rietwijker
Parlevinker 9, tel. 33 13 37

Bachzaal   Concert halls
Bachstraat 3, tel. 73 07 98

Concertgebouw
Van Baerlestraat 98, tel. 71 83 45

Museum Amstelkring
O.Z. Voorburgwal 40, tel. 24 66 04

Schwartze-Huis
Prinsengracht 1091, tel. 22 07 11

Sonesta Koepelzaal
Kattengat 1, tel. 21 22 23

Stedelijk Museum
Paulus Potterstraat 13, tel. 5 73 29 11
From Sept. to May: Saturday afternoon concerts of modern
music

Advance Booking   See entry

Time

Dutch Summertime – i.e. Central European Time (CET) plus
one hour – operates from the beginning of April to the end of
September.

Time to travel

Amsterdam is worth a visit at any time of year, but is especially
attractive in the spring when the parks and bulb-fields are in full
bloom. In the autumn the city and indeed the whole country is
bathed in the same clear light that suffuses the works of the
Dutch Old Masters.

Tipping

In the Netherlands tipping (10–15%) is usually for special services only, but it has become common practice in restaurants,
cafés, hotels and taxis to round up payment to the nearest
guilder.

Tourist Information

See Information

Traffic

Speed limits   The speed limits are 50 kph/31 mph in built-up areas, 80 kph/
50 mph outside built-up areas and for cars with trailers, and
120 kph/75 mph on motorways.
In traffic-calmed areas – indicated by a sign showing a white
house on a blue background – the speed should be no more
than walking pace.

Right of way   In Amsterdam traffic from the right should always be pre-
sumed to have priority. This applies even to the smallest side-

street, and drivers would be well advised to watch out for every
junction, even when on broad main roads.

Main beam or dipped headlights must be used from half an
hour after sunset until one hour before sunrise. During daylight
hours lights must be used if weather conditions make this
necessary. Main beams may not be used in built-up areas if
there is sufficient street lighting, or outside built-up areas when
facing oncoming traffic or following close behind another
vehicle, or if there is street lighting at regular intervals.

Lighting

The legal limit in the Netherlands for alcohol in the blood is 0.5
parts per thousand.

Drinking and driving

Front seat belts must be used if the vehicle is fitted with them.

Seat belts

Amsterdam has at least as many people on bikes as in cars. The
Dutch treat cyclists with great care and consideration, and they
are usually allowed a much bigger safety margin than in other
countries.
Watch out for junctions with cycle tracks where cyclists often
have the right of way.

Bikes in traffic

No parking is allowed on any of the many canal bridges.
Although there are some parking spaces on the edge of the
canals they are nearly always occupied. If you do find one, take
great care when parking or driving away because there is often
nothing to stop you ending up in the water. The Amsterdam
Police tow away cars left parked on pavements.

Parking

See entry

Motoring Assistance

See entry

Petrol

Travel Documents

To enter the Netherlands visitors from Britain and most
Western countries simply require a valid passport (or a British
visitor's passport).

Passports

The Netherlands recognises national driving licences and
vehicle documents, and these should accompany the driver.

Driving licence/vehicle
documents

It is advisable to bring along a green insurance card.

Green card

All visiting foreign cars must carry the international country of
origin sign.

Country of origin

No customs documents are required if the trailer is clearly in
use.

Trailers

No customs documents required.

Bikes and mopeds

Notification must be given of motorboats that can travel faster
than 16 kph/10 mph (possible at large post offices), and they
must have third-party insurance for at least 250 000 hfl.

Motorboats

Water taxis

Amsterdam's water taxis are a good alternative to the con-
ventional version and can be booked on tel.75 09 09.

Water taxis

They have electronic meters and charge on a timed basis. One hour costs about 80 hfl for carrying up to eight people.

Youth Hostels

Stadsdoelen
Kloveniersburgwal 97, tel. 24 68 32
184 beds
Open mid-March–mid-October.

Vondelpark
Zandpad 5, tel. 83 17 44
315 beds
Open all year round

Important Telephone Numbers at a Glance

Emergency Numbers	Telephone Number
AA (London)	09–44–81–954–7373
Ambulance	5 55 55 55
Breakdowns (ANWB patrol service)	06 08 88
Counselling Service for alcohol and drugs	23 78 65
Doctor, Dentist, Chemist (medical emergency)	64 21 11
Fire brigade	21 21 21
Police	22 22 22
RAC (London)	09–44–81–686–2525

	Airlines
Air UK	(010) 37 02 11
Canadian Pacific	22 44 44
KLM	74 77 47
Pan Am	26 20 21
Qantas	83 80 81
SAA/SAL	16 44 44

	Consulates
Australia	(070) 63 09 83
Canada	(070) 61 41 11
South Africa	(070) 92 45 01
United Kingdom	76 43 43
United States of America	79 03 21

	Information
Airport	5 11 04 32
GVB (public transport)	27 27 27
Railway station	23 83 83
Tourist offices	
VVV (tourist information centres)	26 64 44

Lost Property	5 59 91 11
Taxis	77 77 77
Water taxis	75 09 09

Important Telephone Numbers at a Glance

	Telephoning
Information (international calls)	00 18
Operator connected calls	00 10
Dialling codes:	
To Australia	09 61
To Canada	09 1
To South Africa	09 27
To United Kingdom	09 44
To United States of America	09 1
From United Kingdom to Amsterdam	010 31 20

Index

Watch out – there's a thief about!

In Amsterdam you have to take especially good care of your property!
Recent years have seen a steep rise in Amsterdam's crime rate, due to some extent to the drug scene. Hence steel shutters go up in the evening to protect shops even in such crowded shopping streets as Rokin and the Kalverstraat. Unsuspecting tourists are just as likely to fall victim to the criminals as locals. You should be aware of the fact that **muggings** are a possibility at the airport, in the hotel, restaurant or tram, just as much as on the street – where a favourite ploy by pickpockets is to beg in order to find out where you keep your wallet. There is also a very high rate of **thefts from cars**.

You would be very well advised to carry any valuables concealed on your person in a body-belt, or something similar, and should never leave anything in an easily accessible parked car. You should leave the empty glove compartment open and the boot unlocked, and remove the car radio. If you don't it's highly unlikely you'll come back from a short stroll round the town or a sightseeing trip and find anything left in your car.

The Amsterdam **police** are **virtually powerless** to do anything about the many thefts of property. They've long since stopped taking a statement about thefts from cars. You'll find instead that there is a multi-lingual form for you to fill in yourself at the relevant police station. This will then simply be stamped by the appropriate officer for insurance claim purposes.